DEPRESSION AMERICA

DEPRESSION AMERICA

Volume 1

BOOM AND BUST

GROLIER
EDUCATIONAL

About This book

The Great Depression is one of the most important periods of modern U.S. history. Images of breadlines and hungry families are as haunting today as they were at the time. Why did the crisis occur in the world's richest country, and how has it shaped the United States today? *Depression America* answers these questions and reveals a highly complex period in great detail. It describes the uplifting achievements of individuals, tells touching stories of community spirit, and illustrates a rich cultural life stretching from painting to movie-making.

Each of the six volumes covers a particular aspect of the period. The first traces the causes of the Depression through the preceding decades of U.S. history. The second examines the first term of Franklin D. Roosevelt and the New Deal he put in place to temper the effects of the crisis. The third volume studies how the Depression affected the lives of ordinary Americans. Volume 4 reveals the opposition FDR faced from both the political right and left, while Volume 5 explores the effect of the period on U.S. society and culture. The final volume places the Depression in the context of global extremism and the outbreak of World War II, the effects of which restored the United States to economic health.

Each book is split into chapters that explore their themes in depth. References within the text and in a See Also box at the end of each chapter point you to related articles elsewhere in the set, allowing you to further investigate topics of particular interest. There are also many special boxes throughout the set that highlight particular subjects in greater detail. They might provide a biography of an important person, examine the effect of a particular event, or give an eyewitness account of life in the Depression.

If you are not sure where to find a subject, look it up in the set index in each volume. The index covers all six books, so it will help you trace topics throughout the set. A glossary at the end of each book provides a brief explanation of important words and concepts, and a timeline gives a chronological account of key events of the period. The Further Reading list contains numerous books and useful web sites to allow you to do your own research.

Published 2001 by Grolier Educational
Sherman Turnpike
Danbury, Connecticut 06816

© 2001 Brown Partworks Limited

Set ISBN: 0-7172-5502-6
Volume ISBN: 0-7172-5503-4

Library of Congress Cataloging-in-Publication Data
Depression America
    p. cm.
    Includes indexes
    Contents: v. 1. Boom and bust – v. 2. Roosevelt's first term – v. 3. Countryside and city – v. 4. Political tensions – v. 5. U.S. society – v. 6. The war years and economic boom.
    ISBN 0-7172-5502-6 (set : alk. paper)
    1. United States–Economic conditions–1918-1945–Juvenile literature. 3. New Deal, 1933-1939–Juvenile literature. 4. Working class–United States–Juvenile literature. 5. United States–Social life and customs–1918-1945–Juvenile literature. [1. Depressions–1929. 2. New Deal, 1933-1939. 3. United States–History–1919-1933. 4. United States–History– 1933-1945. 5. United States–Economic conditions– 1918-1945.]

HC106.3 D44 2001
330.973'0916–dc21

00-046641

For information address the publisher:
Grolier Educational, Sherman Turnpike, Danbury, Connecticut 06816

Printed and bound in Singapore

For Brown Partworks
Volume consultant:
Prof. Eric Davin, University of Pittsburgh
Managing editor: Tim Cooke
Editors: Claire Ellerton, Edward Horton, Christine Hatt, Lee Stacy
Designers: Sarah Williams, Lynne Ross
Picture research:
Becky Cox, Helen Simm, Daniela Marceddu
Indexer: Kay Ollerenshaw

CONTENTS

1

THE UNITED STATES, 1865-1914

Between the Civil War, which ended in 1865, and World War I, which began in 1914, the United States underwent a crucial change. Americans began to view their world as dynamic and changing, a world where experience and observation empowered innovators, capitalists, and hard-headed business-men as well as the politically astute.

An immigrant family in its Manhattan attic room at the turn of the century. Poverty forced many urban families to live in unsanitary, overcrowded conditions.

between 1860 and 1890 alone—energy, entrepreneurial spirit, and sometimes desperation drove pioneers west across the continent in search of economic opportunity and personal liberty. Meanwhile, economic prosperity brought a clash between two visions of America, both based on traditional political values. Mutualism espoused the importance of the community and a system of "moral capitalism" that worked for the benefit of society as a whole. It was increasingly challenged by faith in the free market, in which there were no restrictions on the activities of individuals or firms.

1. RISE TO ECONOMIC DOMINANCE

In statistical terms the United States' growth was impressive. Industrial production rose by 700 percent from 1865 to 1900, by which time the nation produced

The roots of the Great Depression lay in the economic and industrial system created by American progress by the end of the 19th century. Between the end of the Civil War in 1865 and the time it entered World War I in 1917, the United States rapidly grew to become the world's leading

industrial nation. The sheer speed of the transformation brought problems. Prosperity was far from universal: A few immigrants rose from poverty to great wealth, but the less fortunate remained exploited, with little attention paid to their welfare at work or at home.

As the population rose—it more than doubled to 76 million

An iron mill in Roane, Tennessee. Iron was an essential primary resource for the industrialization of the United States.

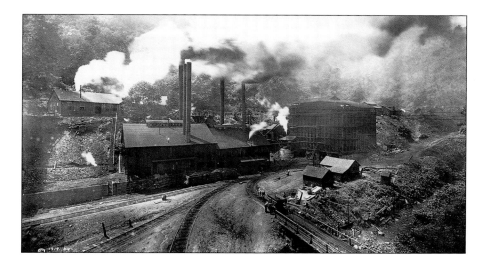

31.9 percent of the world's coal, 34.1 percent of its iron, and 36.7 percent of its steel. The reasons behind this rapid industrial growth were complex, but included the extension of the railroad network and the opening of important new markets in the expanding western territories. The West also provided new resources to fuel development, including coal and iron for industry, and beef and grain to support the growing population.

The increasing numbers of Americans, built in large part on immigrants who labored in the new industries, also drove expansion and the pursuit of ingenious means to increase production. A particularly American faith in commercial success and material wealth added momentum to the process. Many of the pioneers who headed west and those who arrived from Europe were economic migrants, seeking more opportunity and dreaming of economic independence.

THE RAILROADS

Industrialization received a push from the Civil War, when the North's victory was credited partly to its industrial dominance over the South and to its more extensive network of railroads, which allowed it to move troops rapidly. In the postwar world railroad building increased rapidly, with the completion of the first transcontinental line in 1869. Railroads took the lead in pushing the frontier west toward the Pacific coast. Only an eighth of the newly opened land went to farmers, the rest to speculators

and the railroads, who were awarded generous concessions.

In the 1880s, the peak decade of railroad building, around 93,000 miles (150,000 km) of track were laid. By the end of the century railroads united the country, stretching from New York to California and Washington State, from the swamps of Florida to the mountains of Wyoming.

Wherever the railroad went, new communities formed or old ones expanded. Urbanization provided new markets and caused a division in attitudes that would split the rural and urban populations for decades. By 1901 some 40 American cities had more than 100,000 citizens, while four families in every 10 lived in cities. The overwhelming majority of the population remained rural.

THE MATERIALS FOR INDUSTRY

In the South cotton was still king. Although production was heavily mechanized, the industry still remained reliant on the labor of many thousands of badly paid workers, white and black alike. Despite the effort to reshape society during Reconstruction, Jim Crow laws kept the region's black citizens impoverished.

From the plantations the bales of cotton were shipped north by rail or south by river to ports such as New Orleans, and then to northern cotton mills or to Europe. In the great mills ranks of automated, steam-powered jennies, spindles, and looms turned the cotton into fine cloth.

Timber from the eastern woodlands and the Northwest was used for construction, especially of

The West

The West provided new sources of foods to support expansion. From Texas and the prairies trains brought beef to cities such as Chicago, whose stockyards and processing plants saw it grow from a frontier outpost to a thriving city in a few decades. Grain followed the same eastward route, often harvested on a large scale by machinery. Improvements in canning and refrigeration made it even easier to transport perishable foodstuffs to markets over long distances.

Elevators at river ports, like these in Buffalo, New York, were collection points for American grain before it was shipped abroad.

THE FINANCIAL WORLD AND THE GROWTH OF TRUSTS

As industry grew, so did the importance of the banks that supported it. The Rockefellers, who owned Standard Oil, deposited their vast earnings—$40 to $60 million a year—in the National City Bank of James Stillman. Jacob H. Schiff ran the Kuhn, Loeb, and Company investment bank, while J. Pierpoint Morgan (1837–1913) presided over the bank that bore his name.

America's business leaders had begun early a trend toward amalgamating firms to create significant concentrations of economic power in the hands of a few citizens. Business monopolies, where there was only one supplier in a market, were banned by federal law; but manufacturers cooperated by forming trusts, which brought together similar companies in umbrella organizations that remained nominally independent

Mechanization of agriculture—these machines are helping with the harvest in the Midwest—allowed U.S. farmers to produce far larger amounts of food.

the railroads themselves and of the communities that emerged in the West, while coal from Virginia and the Appalachian Mountains powered the locomotives. Coal was essential, too, for the industry that turned iron into a workable metal or into stronger, more flexible steel. From cities like Pittsburgh and the furnaces and steel mills that grew up along the waterways of the East came rails for the railroads, girders for new skyscrapers, molds to make machine tools that would make more machines, pins and needles, and gun metal to cast the Colt .45 revolver—the so-called Peacemaker that tamed the West.

Inventions

Industrial expansion and individual ingenuity inspired many significant inventions, including:
Sleeping car 1864
Air brake 1872
Commercial typewriter, 1873
Telephone 1876
Lightbulb 1879
Skyscraper 1883–1885
Photographic film 1884
Coca-Cola 1886
Mass-produced camera 1888
Zipper c.1890

Getting Rich

The last quarter of the 19th century was a golden age of railroad construction in the United States. Some five parallel routes across the continent had been studied in the middle of the century. The first to be built, the Union Pacific in 1869, ran roughly along the 41st Parallel. When it opened, however, customers had little demand for its services. Only one train a week in either direction was enough to cope with the number of passengers. In 1885, however, when demand increased with migration to the Midwest, the Plains states, and California, the Santa Fe Railroad and the Northern Pacific Railway both reached the West Coast, at Los Angeles and Puget Sound respectively. In 1910 Western Pacific opened the last transcontinental line, to Oakland, California.

The growth of the transcontinental lines was matched by efforts by the main railroad companies to create networks that would link the regions of the West: The Union Pacific emerged dominant.

Grand Central Station under construction in New York between 1905 and 1910. The station remains the city's major railroad terminal.

but, in the eyes of critics, operated like monopolies. Such trusts could keep prices high, for example, or force their suppliers to lower their prices. Prominent trusts included the major railroad companies and

•

"Get money.… Get it dishonestly if you can, honestly if you must."

•

J. D. Rockefeller's Standard Oil, formed in 1882.

While trust supporters pointed at the lower overheads that allowed them to reduce prices, for the people who opposed the concentration of economic power, the men who ran the trusts were "robber barons," growing rich by exploiting others. In the 1870s the humorist Mark Twain lumped together business practices with corruption in local and federal government when he said: "Get money. Get it quickly. Get it in abundance. Get it in prodigious abundance. Get it dishonestly if you can, honestly if you must."

2. THE PRINCIPLES AND MORALS OF BUSINESS

The injustice of a system that concentrated economic and political power in the hands of so few people led to protest by those who advocated a mutualist approach based on the importance of community. Others justified the system or even celebrated the type of rags-to-riches opportunity it seemed to offer. Novelist Horatio Alger (1832–1899) sold 20 million books in the late 19th century based on rags-to-riches tales. Alger wrote more than 100 novels

about the rise of Ragged Dick, Tattered Tom, and other bootblacks, foundlings, and runaways who, through perseverance, hard work, honesty, cheerfulness, and luck achieve wealth and fame.

Many Americans believed that the right of the individual to do more or less as he or she pleased lay at the heart of the country's

•

"It is merely the working out of a law of nature and a law of God."

•

political philosophy. Others pointed to precedents of federal intervention in the economy, like the building of the National Road in the 1820s and the more recent encouragement of railroad building through land grants. They called for government intervention to deal with the worst negative effects of capitalism.

SOCIAL DARWINISM
Many free-market advocates saw the business world as an expression of a natural law, Social Darwinism. Social Darwinism, advocated in England by Herbert Spencer (1820–1903) and in the United States by Yale professor William Graham Sumner (1840–1910), applied the theories of Charles Darwin to human society.

Darwin's theory of evolution was based on the idea of natural selection, or survival of the fittest. In other words, those members of a species best suited to their environment would come to dominate at the expense of less well-adapted specimens. Spencer predicted that a similar economic process would inevitably lead to American progress: "The American nation will be a long time in evolving its ultimate form, but… its ultimate form will be high."

The victims—the "unfittest"— would be the unavoidable price of such progress. William Sumner went so far as to speculate that the slum dwellers of America's cities actually enjoyed their way of life and should therefore not be helped: "The evidence is that they like the life, and are indifferent to what others consider its evils and discomforts."

Industrialists such as Andrew Carnegie (1835–1919) seized on Social Darwinism as a justification of their power: They had, one argued, "superior ability, foresight, and adaptability." John D. Rockefeller (1839–1937) saw his own success as inevitable: "It is merely the working out of a law of nature and a law of God."

A cotton plantation in Tennessee. Cotton depended on manual labor for its harvest, but its processing was increasingly mechanized.

Social Darwinism and Government
In government, too, Social Darwinism struck a chord with politicians raised on laissez-faire, the belief that the economy should regulate itself. Although such a belief had never been unchallenged, American history had precedents for it in Jeffersonian liberalism. Such currents of think-

European Attitudes

Herbert Spencer's emphasis on the individual over society was more popular in the United States than in his native England, where legislation regulated workers' hours and helped the poor. Elsewhere, in Germany the government introduced a social security system. Spencer argued against all such intervention in the economy and against public sanitation, housing regulation, taxes, and other government measures.

Rags to Riches?

One of the reasons some Americans supported the idea of free enterprise was that it seemed to work. In their interpretation economic and territorial expansion created a fluid society in which people could improve their own lives and social status. There were a few examples of celebrated individuals who had risen from lowly roots in a way that would have been almost impossible in other countries.

Inventor Thomas Edison (1847–1931), for example, went to school for just three months before he became a railroad newsboy at age 12. Andrew Carnegie (1835–1919) had emigrated with his family from Scotland in 1848 to find work. After working as a bobbin boy in a cotton mill and attending night school, Carnegie became a messenger in a telegraph office and then assistant to a railroad manager. Six years later Carnegie replaced his boss as superintendent. Carnegie increased his wealth through investments in iron mills, railroad plants, and an oilfield. At the age of about 40 he founded a steel mill. It was the first step in a process that would bring him control of much of the U.S. steel industry and make him the world's richest man.

Edison and Carnegie were exceptions, however. No matter how much contemporaries trumpeted the myth that the United States was "the land of opportunity," an analysis of American business leaders toward the end of the 19th century shows that in virtually all cases they had actually been born wealthy.

ing would become evident again in Herbert Hoover's reaction to the Wall Street Crash of 1929 and the Great Depression in the early 1930s (see Chapter 7, "Hoover: The Search for a Solution").

In 1887, when President Grover Cleveland (1837–1908) vetoed the supply of free seed to drought-stricken farmers in Texas, he explained what was then the dominant philosophy of his own Democratic Party and what has, at various times, been the fundamental principle of Republicans and Democrats alike: "I do not believe that the power and duty of the General Government ought to be extended to the relief of individual suffering which is in no manner properly related to the public

service or benefit.... The lesson should constantly be enforced that though the people support the Government, Government should not support the people."

The Duty of the Rich

Andrew Carnegie was the world's richest man—on one deal in 1910 he made $300 million. When he died in 1919, he was worth only $22 million, having given away most of his money to causes such as the building of libraries and the promotion of peace studies. Carnegie, who wrote, "The man who dies thus rich dies disgraced," summed up the attitudes of some of the rich, who accepted that they had a moral duty to help the

A child worker photographed at the Globe Cotton Mill, Augusta, Ga., by Lewis Wicks Hine. Hine was one of numerous reformers who militated for social improvements around the turn of the century.

less fortunate. In Carnegie's case those attitudes reflected the mutualistic ethos of his working-class youth, when people had looked out for one another. His grandfather had been jailed as a Chartist,

John Dewey (1859–1952) argued for what was called pragmatism. Pragmatism dismissed the idea that business expressed a natural law. It proposed that people could change their own environment

mainly the railroads on which they depended to transport their produce. Supported by labor, small business, and consumers, the influence of the farmers forced the rural states of the Midwest to pass legislation in the 1880s to limit the power of the railroad corporations

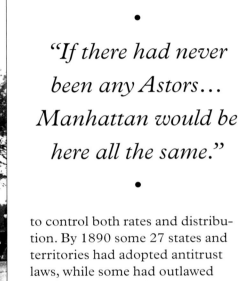

•

"If there had never been any Astors… Manhattan would be here all the same."

•

to control both rates and distribution. By 1890 some 27 states and territories had adopted antitrust laws, while some had outlawed monopolies altogether.

The Sherman Antitrust Act
Because trusts operated across state boundaries, federal law was necessary to control them. In

A library in Washington, D.C., built with money from Andrew Carnegie, the world's richest man.

a member of a group advocating reform in England in the 1840s.

Carnegie was not the only philanthropist. John D. Rockefeller and his son, John Junior, gave away $1.5 billion to medical research and black education. The rich were quick to condemn wastefulness. In the depression of the 1890s the Bradley Martin family spent $370,000 on a ball. Condemnation by New York society forced them to flee to Europe.

CRITICISM OF BUSINESS PRACTICES
The laissez-faire doctrine did not go unchallenged. Thinkers such as William James (1842–1910) and

through social improvement. Lester Frank Ward (1841–1913) argued for social planning and the provision of welfare. Thorstein Veblen (1857–1929) mocked the claimed superiority of the rich.

Opposition to unbridled capitalism also came from observers, often the owners of small or medium businesses, who saw the trusts that dominated business not as a stabilizing influence on the economy, as their supporters claimed, but as a disruptive one. From inside and outside industry people protested the power of the trusts to control prices. They blamed Rockefeller's Standard Oil for a collapse in the price of crude oil in the late 1870s, for example.

Farmers were also quick to join the antitrust movement, attacking

Henry George

Economist Henry George (1839–1897) argued that many of America's millionaires owed their wealth not to superior talents but to lucky increases in the value of land. George said that "No human being can produce or lay up land. If the Astors had all remained in Germany, or if there had never been any Astors, the land of Manhattan Island would have been here all the same."

A full-length portrait of John D. Rockefeller, one of the American elite who justified their privilege by their "superior ability."

1890 the Sherman Antitrust Act marked a new degree of federal intervention in business affairs. The act made illegal all monopolies, combinations, and attempts to restrain free interstate trade and competition. Although the law was a landmark, the government's reluctance to enforce it made it ineffective. By 1901 only 18 antitrust cases had been taken to court, none serious. By contrast, the main victims of the act turned out to be not the trusts but the unions that aimed to represent their workers.

POPULAR PROTEST

Important support for the mutualistic tradition came from the working class via the labor movement. The Knights of Labor emerged as the most important working-class organization of the 19th century. Originally a secret society, the Knights advocated a system of workers' cooperatives to replace capitalism and argued that industrial workers shared common interests with other economic producers, such as farmers and storekeepers.

The Knights abandoned secrecy in 1879, when Terence Powderly (1849–1924) became leader. Powderly was reluctant to instigate potentially violent strikes or other overt action against employers, preferring to boycott nonunion firms and maintain a propaganda campaign. Powderly's approach was rejected by many of the organization's regional leaders, who continued supporting more active protest.

The Knights grew rapidly. Between 1869 and 1896 more than 15,000 locals were formed and three million workers initiated as members. Over half of all American towns with a population bigger than 1,000 had a chapter; there were also chapters in Canada, New Zealand, Australia, and Europe.

Strikes and Violence

The most dramatic manifestations of the struggle for America's soul between mutualism and capitalist individualism came in a series of violent labor disputes. In the Pennsylvania coalfields in the 1870s a secret society named the Molly Maguires was blamed for murdering company officials. In 1877 a strike on the Baltimore and Ohio Railroad grew into the biggest strike anywhere in the world during the 19th century. There was serious unrest in Pittsburgh, Chicago, and throughout the north. Troops were called in to fire on the strikers.

In 1886 in the so-called Haymarket Riot a bomb thrown at a strikers' meeting in Chicago killed a policeman. The police arrested 200 anarchists, who opposed the whole system of U.S. government, and charged 31 people with conspiracy to murder: Four were later hanged. In the mind of the public the affair confirmed that much labor activity was part of an anarchist plot to overthrow capitalism. When Powderly failed to show solidarity with the accused men members began to desert the Knights of Labor. By 1893 membership had fallen to only 75,000.

In 1892 another great industrial confrontation came at the steel mills of Homestead, Pennsylvania. Owner Andrew Carnegie and his manager Henry Clay Frick (1849–1919) defeated the Amalgamated Association of Iron, Steel, and Tin Workers, one of the country's strongest unions. The union kept up the price of labor and asked for raises when the bosses introduced new machinery to make the mill the most modern in the country.

When the union rejected proposed wage cuts, Frick locked all 3,500 employees out of the factory. He built a 3-mile-long fence around it, complete with searchlights and shooting holes, and planned to replace the workers with cheaper nonunion labor protected by Pinkerton detectives. When the Pinkertons tried to land by boat inside the plant, an all-day gun battle broke out that left nine steelmen and seven Pinkertons dead and 163 people seriously injured before the trapped detectives surrendered.

The Democratic state governor broke the lockout with 8,000 militiamen, who escorted nonunion workers into the plant a week later. In the first real confrontation between a modern corporation and an organized union, labor—and the mutualist tradition—had suffered a reverse that would last until the 1930s. The strike leaders were prosecuted for treason, though none were convicted. Carnegie remarked, "Life is worth living again."

In 1894 the American Railway Union, led by Eugene V. Debs (1855–1926), ran a strike against the Pullman Company to help workers whose wages had been cut by a third in the depression of the early 1890s, leaving them about 76 cents a day for food and clothing. A boycott against the company spread to 27 states. Newspapers railed against Debs as a dictator and condemned the strike as "socialist pestilence brought here from abroad by the criminals and outcasts of European slums."

Attorney General Richard Olney (1835–1917) invoked the 1890 Sherman Antitrust Act—originally enacted to diminish rather than support the interests of big business—arguing that the union was an outlawed combination. President Grover Cleveland sent 2,000 troops to Chicago, with 5,000 marshals and 3,500 deputies employed by the railroads. He announced, "If it takes the entire army and navy of the United States to deliver a postal card in Chicago, that card will be delivered." In the riots that followed, 34 men died, the ARU was broken, and Eugene Debs went to prison for contempt.

Cleveland's famous postal card declaration was no more than a pretext to break the union. The strikers had always allowed mail trains to pass. The president's intervention was an important factor in the Democratic defeat in the presidential election of 1896.

THE KIND OF ANTI-TRUST LEGISLATION THAT IS NEEDED.
Uncle Sam—You 've a powerful big man, and you dark?—Open up those books!   have your suns. But if you 're honest why do you hide in the

THE FARMERS' VOICE

A parallel protest against individualist capitalism came from the same farmers who supported the antitrust campaign. Farmers had a poor time. From 1860 to 1890 there was a 50 percent fall in the prices of wheat and cotton. Meanwhile the cost of farmers' mortgages doubled.

In Lampasas County, Texas, in 1877, farmers formed the Southern Alliance. In little over a decade the movement became a National Farmers' Alliance with half a million members in the South and 100,000 in Kansas alone. Alliance speaking tours

Uncle Sam shines the light of congressional investigation to illuminate "King Trusts" in this cartoon from 1902. Despite such optimism, trusts remained largely untouched by legal challenges.

reached some two million farmers in 43 states. Speakers wanted to bring the railroads under public ownership, to shorten the working day, and to establish a "democratic money system" of warehouses where farmers could borrow credit against deposits of grain, releasing money into the rural economy.

The Alliance enjoyed local success, and in 1892 its supporters

Bryan's Appeal

Democratic leader William Jennings Bryan appealed to concerns directly linked to Populist ideals when he told his party in 1896: "You come to us and tell us that the great cities are in favor of the gold standard; we reply that the great cities stand upon our broad and fertile prairies. Burn down your cities and leave our farms, and your cities will spring up again as if by magic; but destroy our farms and the grass will grow in the streets of every city in the land." And again, "You shall not press down upon the brow of labor this crown of thorns, you shall not crucify mankind upon a cross of gold."

founded a national equivalent, the People's Party, commonly known as the Populist Party. The party, the largest popular movement in U.S. political history, appealed for social justice for the millions overlooked by the agendas of the Republicans and Democrats. Its program included government ownership of railroads and other communications, a graduated income tax, a secret ballot in elections, protection for labor unions, and restrictions on immigration. It called for cheap credit and a national currency linked to silver rather than gold.

In the presidential election of 1892 the Populist candidate, General James Weaver (1833–1912), won about 10 percent of the vote and carried five states. Over the next few years the Populists effectively wiped out the Democratic Party west of the Mississippi. In the east Populists often ran on the same ticket as Democrats, and by the 1896 election the Populists were largely absorbed into the Democratic Party. Their influence continued, however. The reformist tendencies that emerged in the early 20th century in both the Democratic and Republican parties were heavily influenced by Populist philosophy.

THE DEPRESSION OF 1893

In 1893 a financial panic and a rush to buy gold began a depression that lasted until 1897. Around 600 banks closed, along with 15,000 companies, while 56 railroads went bankrupt. Two in every five Americans were out of work. In 1894 Jacob Coxey (1854–1951) led 10,000 unem-

ployed men, dubbed "Coxey's Army," in a march on Washington, D.C. They asked for mutualist-inspired legislation to provide funds for communities to pay the unemployed to work on public works projects.

As one way to protect jobs, the nativist movement reemerged to protest against immigration. Previously its main targets had been the Irish; now the Irish joined the protests against workers from southern and eastern Europe. Senator Henry Cabot Lodge (1850–1924) advocated a literacy test to weed out "dangerous elements." Future president

A caricature of three U.S. capitalists shows, from left, J. Pierpoint Morgan, Andrew Mellon, and John D. Rockefeller.

Life in the Cities

For the poor of America's cities, many of whom were newly arrived immigrants, living conditions were often terrible. As New York police commissioner (1895–1897) and governor (1899–1900), future president Theodore Roosevelt witnessed at first hand the conditions of the city's poorest citizens. Early each morning he had toured the slums of the city with the Danish-born crusading journalist and photographer Jacob Riis (1849–1914). Of all the city slums the most notorious were on the Lower East Side, home to Irish, Germans, Italians, and Jews. They lived in "rookeries" such as Mulberry Bend in a maze of stinking courts and alleys in tenements that might be four to eight stories tall. Riis recorded one tenement with 132 rooms that housed 1,324 Italians. In one 12-foot-by-12-foot room lived five families with 20 people, sharing two beds. Some of the city's 1.2 million tenement dwellers were better off than others. The poorest families had to save money by renting cellars, which were cheaper, or rooms with no windows or ventilation at all. Riis found a Russian Jewish family living in a hutch beneath a staircase.

With no other way to accommodate the influx of newcomers, the New York City authorities simply dropped their minimum legal space requirement for housing from 600 cubic feet per person to 400 for adults and 200 for children. Although the building of rooms with no windows was outlawed in 1894, the law only applied to new buildings and did nothing to change the old ones. Some 40 percent of all tenement dwellers suffered from tuberculosis. Living mainly on bread and potatoes, without running water or indoor toilets, tenement dwellers were also prey to certain diseases. Cities had high mortality rates from typhoid; Pittsburgh, Pa., introduced water filtration in 1896 to combat the problem, and the number of deaths declined.

Riis's photographs and writings, most notably his famous 1890 book *How the Other Half Lives*, forced the New York authorities into numerous changes to improve social conditions. They pulled down Mulberry Bend and replaced it with more sanitary housing. In 1908, however, tenement slums were still common in the city. On the Lower West Side even Trinity Church was a slum landlord, owning 500 rotting tenements between Greenwich Village and Canal Street, before a magazine campaign embarrassed the church into razing them.

An immigrant mother and her children, with a baby nearby, pick nuts in their Manhattan tenement in 1911. Such badly paid work was often undertaken by immigrant families in order to supplement any money the father or mother could earn outside the home.

Woodrow Wilson (1856–1924), often remembered today as a liberal, described the incomers in 1902 as "men out of the ranks where there was neither skill nor energy, nor any initiative of quick intelligence...."

Morgan and the Railroads

As would happen in the Great Depression, some people found opportunity in economic crisis. J. Pierpoint Morgan rescued railroads from receivership by advancing cash to their directors in return for what was termed "Morganization," a program of cost cutting and consolidation of routes in which stockholders were forced to accept lower rates of

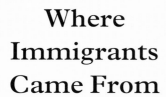

Where Immigrants Came From

After the 1890s the traditional sources of emigration from northern and western Europe changed. By the outbreak of World War I in 1914, around 80 percent of newcomers were from southern and eastern Europe and Asia Minor, including Poles, Ukrainians, Slovaks, and other Slavs, Hungarians, Italians, Greeks, and Turks, along with Jews from Russia, Poland, and Romania. Across the Pacific came smaller numbers of Chinese, Japanese, and Filipinos. From the American continent many Canadians and Mexicans made their way into the United States.

interest. In this way Morgan got control of more than 15 percent of the nation's railroads, imposing order for the benefit of his own shareholders. The process marked a new degree of power for money-men rather than the industrialists who had previously put business blocks together.

Bryan's Democrats

In the election of 1896 the Democratic candidate chosen to replace Grover Cleveland was William Jennings Bryan (1860–1925), who united a party split between those who wanted the dollar linked to the gold standard and those who believed it should be tied to silver.

Bryan's awakening of what he perceived as old agrarian values of social justice made him the leader of a Democratic Party committed to reform for the next 16 years. His idealism to some extent found its eventual fruition in the social and economic programs of the New Deal in the 1930s. Bryan lost the election, however, defeated largely by his lack of support in the cities

Laundry in a New York tenement yard gives a graphic illustration of the crowded conditions of the people who lived within.

and by industrialists' threat to bring the country to its knees in the event of a Democrat victory.

McKinley and Empire

In 1896 the Republican William McKinley (1843–1901) became president. The five years before he was killed by an anarchist in 1901 represented the peak of capitalism in the United States. Mutualism had largely been defeated by the supporters of free-market individualism. Big business boomed. The public increasingly invested in the stock market: In January 1901 the New York Stock Exchange experienced two million deals in a day for the first time; the first three-million-deal day came four months later.

Under McKinley the trusts reached their peak. In 1901 J. P. Morgan united the whole steel business, from mines and mills to manufacturers, in one huge

A U.S. Empire

During McKinley's presidency America became an imperial power. In 1898, aided by fervor whipped up by the press, the United States acted on a pretext to go to war with Spain in Cuba. A quickly won victory left the United States in possession of the Philippines and Puerto Rico; the same year it annexed the naval base of Hawaii in the Pacific. Quite what the Americans should do with their empire was another matter. McKinley admitted that there was no better reason to take control of the Philippines than a lack of acceptable alternatives.

THE IMMIGRANT.

organization. He bought out the steel production operations of Andrew Carnegie to form the world's first billion-dollar firm, the United States Steel Corporation. Morgan now controlled half the nation's steel production.

3. AMERICA'S POOR AND SOCIAL REFORM

The turn of the century brought pressure from reformers to improve the lives of those missing out on the American dream. Among them were the farmers of the Midwest and the poor laborers of the South. The millions of workers who supported the great industries suffered from appalling conditions at work and at home.

IMMIGRANTS

Many of those who endured the worst conditions were America's immigrants. In the 50 years from the end of the Civil War to 1915 more than 26 million immigrants arrived in the United States, an average of 10,000 a week. The incoming population boomed in the 1880s, fell off during the depression of the 1890s, when anti-immigrant "nativist" agitation was at its height, and reached its peak in the first decade of the new century. In 1907, the busiest year, 1,285,349 people arrived. Many did not intend to stay, however. Virtually all the Chinese and half the Italians arriving were seeking only to earn money before returning home. Nevertheless, probably around 20 million new Americans stayed in the country. In 1908 Jewish playwright Israel Zangwill (1864–1926) first coined the description of the United States as "the great Melting Pot."

For contemporary Americans, descended themselves from earlier waves of immigrants, the newcomers were not always welcome. Economic depressions brought an upsurge in nativist sentiment against immigrants; they also saw immigration almost stop. In reality, labor organizations reported that in around 75 percent of industries immigrants had little negative

This cartoon—torn and repaired since it was published in 1903—questions the value of the immigrant to America, showing both positive and negative points.

effect on jobs, although unions condemned their use as strikebreakers in industrial disputes. Contemporaries accused steamship lines of drumming up business by promising immigrants jobs and wealth in the United States, but in fact there was little such enticement, though new prepayment arrangements did make buying tickets easier.

Immigrants and Labor

Economic grounds lay behind much emigration from Europe. There, the population was growing at the same time as traditional society was collapsing in the face of cheap grain imports from North and South America and upheavals such as the decline of feudal society in Austria-Hungary and Russia. Ongoing industrialization also caused social upheaval. The same economic desperation that drove European peasants and small farmers across the Atlantic sent many more into the cities of their own continent.

In the United States the vast majority of immigrants settled in the cities of the Northeast. Few had the capital to set up in agriculture; most were drawn instead to the wages available from urban industry and the security of settling near their own country-people. Nationalities established support networks or dominated life in a particular area of a city. By 1910 over two-thirds of people in the 12 largest cities were either foreign-born or the children of immigrants. Chicago had more Poles than Warsaw and more Czechs than Prague.

By the turn of the century the workforce in every American industry was dominated by immigrants, often enabled to do unskilled work by the automation of industrial processes. In many cases different nationalities concentrated in specific trades. East European Jews worked in textiles and clothing, Italians in construction, while Slovaks, Poles, and Hungarians labored in mining. Immigrant children followed their parents, often working from an early age to supplement the family income. Child labor was not entirely an immigrant problem: It existed throughout the South, where there were very few immigrants.

ROOSEVELT AND THE PROGRESSIVES

The U.S. workforce was one of the least protected in the Western world. Industrial work was hard, dirty, and boring. Conditions were often overcrowded and unsanitary. Adults and children might work up to 16 hours a day. As the gulf widened between employers and employed, labor relations grew more organized.

Labor's campaign to protect America's industrial workers

seemed to face promising circumstances during the presidency of Theodore Roosevelt (1858–1919) from 1901 to 1909. During the so-called Progressive Era politicians from both major parties sought to address the ills of society. The experiment was not a complete success. By the end of the decade children still labored in factories,

Workers and the Law

The United States lagged behind European countries in health and safety legislation that limited working hours, required safety guards around machines, or prohibited the employment of children. Industrial accidents were common—around 30,000 people a year died by 1910, and 500,000 were injured—but the United States was the last industrialized country to provide compensation for people injured at work.

A demonstration in New York City staged in 1914 by the Industrial Workers of the World. Mistrust of the aims of the Wobblies led even many workers to regard them with suspicion.

workers could still be arrested for their political opinions, and the poor still lived in privation.

Roosevelt started his term in a pugnacious mood. In 1901, one modern commentator believes, 20 powerful men controlled America. In 1902 Roosevelt took on one of them head on. J. Pierpoint Morgan had just combined the holdings of two railroads to form Northern Securities, which controlled all transportation between the Great Lakes and the Northwest. Roosevelt prosecuted Morgan under the Sherman Antitrust Act. One newspaper observed, "Wall Street is paralyzed at the thought that a president of the United States should sink so low as to enforce the law." Roosevelt won, however, and in 1904 the trust was broken up.

In the election the same year Roosevelt was returned with an increased majority. Although he prosecuted other trusts, in later years he came to believe that trusts

The original cover of The Jungle *by Upton Sinclair. Sinclair's novel was important in highlighting poor working conditions in many of America's industries.*

railroad rates and to supervise health standards in the Pure Food and Drug Act. Roosevelt was too radical for Congress, however, and too autocratic for many Congressmen. In addition, many blamed him for a financial panic that shook Wall Street in 1907.

The activities of social reformers such as the muckrakers and others kept up the pressure for reform. Upton Sinclair (1878–1968), later a famous novelist, recorded in *The Jungle* the story of an immigrant working in Chicago's meatpacking district in terrible conditions. Susan B. Anthony

(1820–1906) and her supporters militated for suffrage; and some, such as Florence Kelley (1859–1932), advocated social reforms aimed at women. When Kelley achieved these reforms as chief factory inspector in Illinois, the Supreme Court overturned them, arguing that they offended employers' rights as property owners. Lewis Wicks Hine (1874–1940) photographed young children working in industry.

Like the conservative Congress that thwarted Roosevelt, the overthrow of Kelley's reforms was a reminder of the forces against change. Federal authorities continued to support what some people saw as free opportunity, others as the interests of big business. Legal decisions favored employers over employees. When a new law as late as 1916 made it

William Howard Taft, addressing a meeting during his presidency, alienated noninterventionists with his support of tariffs.

were not inherently bad. Only those that operated unfairly should be broken up.

Roosevelt's Reforms

Roosevelt, the "trust-buster," set himself up as the arbiter of a "square deal" between corporations, labor, and the people, acknowledging the government's role in the marketplace. He mediated a coal strike in 1902, for example. In his second term, supported by a more reformist Congress after the 1906 elections, he instituted social reforms and also changes to business practices. He enacted laws to regulate

illegal to employ children under the age of 14, it was ruled unconstitutional two years later.

THE WOBBLIES

The Industrial Workers of the World was formed in 1905 to provide a union for America's unskilled workers, many of them immigrants. Under the leadership of "Big Bill" Haywood (1869–1928) the Wobblies, as members were known, proposed a program of radical socialism that would be ushered in by a general strike.

The small group—they were probably only 150,000 strong—instilled great fear and met with stern punishment. In 1909 a Wobbly was sentenced to a month's hard labor for reading out the Declaration of Independence to assert his right to free speech. In 1912 police with clubs attacked women and children during a strike at Lawrence, Massachusetts. The following year militia and federal troops broke a strike at a Colorado mine owned by the Rockefellers at the cost of over 100 lives, including again women and children. Such a situation ill became an era that was generally celebrated as "progressive." The Wobblies survived, however, until they were finally smashed for their opposition to the United States entering World War I in 1917.

TAFT'S PRESIDENCY

In 1909 Roosevelt stepped down, and the presidency passed to Republican William Howard Taft (1857–1930), who found it difficult to unite his divided party and live in his predecessor's shadow. Taft prosecuted more trusts than Roosevelt had done, introduced the income tax at the demand of rural voters, and limited federal workers to an eighthour day, but his progressive reputation was damaged by his support of increased tariffs. Such a policy aligned Taft with old-school Republicans rather than Roosevelt's progressives. Taft alienated many of his supporters.

In 1912 Roosevelt challenged for the Republican Party nomination. He lost to Taft and responded by forming his own Progressive Party. The Democratic Party meanwhile, was now led by another progressive thinker who had taken the place of William Jennings Bryan. He was Woodrow Wilson (1856–1924), a man determined to redress some of America's economic imbalance. In the election Wilson, Roosevelt, and a third candidate with progressive views—ex-union boss and Socialist leader Eugene V. Debs—polled more than 75 percent of the vote. Roosevelt and Taft split Republican supporters, and Wilson was elected with a minority of the vote.

The Triangle Shirtwaist Fire

Public opinion swung behind labor in 1911. On March 25 a fire broke out at the Triangle Shirtwaist Company on the eighth to tenth floors of a New York building. Fireladders only reached the sixth floor, and the workers, mainly young Italian and Jewish women, were trapped. The owners kept the doors to the stairs locked to prevent theft. Some 46 people died jumping from the building; another 100 burned to death. In the wake of the disaster a state commission investigated many businesses and passed laws limiting the working week for women and children to 54 hours and introducing industrial compensation for injured workers for the first time.

Muckrakers

Among agitators for reform were a group of journalists whom Roosevelt dubbed "muckrakers" for a character in the religious allegory *The Pilgrim's Progress*. Ida Tarbell (1857–1944) exposed the corruption and coercion behind Standard Oil, while Lincoln Steffens (1866–1936) photographed the ledger in Minneapolis that recorded illegal payments, or graft, to councilmen. Ray Stannard Baker (1870–1946) exposed unfair practices by both unions and employers. However, the muckrakers were condemned as sentimentalists even by Progressives such as Roosevelt himself.

2

THE UNITED STATES IN WORLD WAR I, 1914-1918

When Europe went to war in 1914, the United States remained neutral. When the war began to affect U.S. ships, citizens, and trade, however, the neutrality policy changed. With the support of many Americans—and the opposition of others—Woodrow Wilson led his country into the conflict.

Shortly after 8:30 P.M. on the evening of April 2, 1917, the recently reelected U.S. president, Virginia-born former professor of history Woodrow Wilson, rose to address an extraordinary session of Congress. Speaking to the assembled members of the House of Representatives and Senate in a manner described by one witness as "solemn and burdened," Wilson asked them to back his decision that the United States should declare war on Germany.

Wilson's request directly contradicted the policy of strict neutrality that he himself had announced to the Senate on August 19, 1914, shortly after the outbreak of the conflict in Europe. Then, Wilson had stated that the country must remain "neutral in fact as well as in name during these days that are to try men's souls."

Now, little more than 30 months later, Wilson urged Congress to "formally accept the status of belligerent which has been thrust upon it [by Germany]." The president was asking

•

"...neutral in fact as well as name during these days that are to try men's souls."

•

Congress to support his decision to back the Allies, led by Britain, France, Italy, and Russia, in their war against the forces of Austria-Hungary, Bulgaria, Germany, and Turkey, known collectively as the Central Powers.

Wilson's new position provoked much opposition from politicians and citizens who questioned the United States' involvement in a European conflict, from those opposed to war itself, and from the substantial portion of Americans of German extraction. Eventually the president had his way. On April 4 the Senate backed a declaration of war by a ratio of 13 to 1, the House of Representatives by 6 to 1. The two decisive votes marked the conclusion of the major shift in the country's foreign policy from neutrality to military intervention between 1914 and 1917. The change in policy had an effect on U.S. domestic politics throughout and after the war.

1. WILSON IN POWER
As Europe moved toward war in the summer of 1914, after a long period of military tension between the main combatants, few Americans, from the president to the average citizen, saw any reason for the United States to become

involved. Many people perceived the conflict as a purely European affair brought about by the political, economic, and military rivalries of the leading world powers of the time. Most Americans had more pressing concerns. They centered on the state of the nation itself and its role as a major power in the Caribbean, Central America, and the Pacific, questions that had dominated U.S. foreign and economic policy since America had founded its empire in 1898 (see Chapter 1, "The United States, 1865–1914").

Wilson, a progressive Democrat, had been elected in 1912 on a ticket of moderate liberal domestic reform and the maintenance of American hegemony in its recently established spheres of influence.

WILSON'S DOMESTIC POLICY

The chief thrust of Wilson's domestic policy was to regulate and reform the nation's rapidly changing social and economic life. He needed to balance the aspirations and needs of an increasingly wealthy and educated urban population with those of a struggling farming community and various pressure groups, such as prohibitionists and suffragists, and small businesses opposed to the powerful corporations that dominated the U.S. economy. Such corporations—some 300 effectively ran 40 percent of the country's manufacturing base—had brought the country prosperity. They continued to dominate several foreign markets, particularly in Latin America and the Caribbean, to the benefit of the economy as a whole. Wilson's challenge was to curtail the worst monopolistic excesses of these corporations without destroying

the bedrock of the economy, while also satisfying to some degree the radical political voices calling for deep-seated domestic reform.

MAJOR LEGISLATION

Wilson's early presidency introduced a number of pieces of legislation relating to the economy. In 1913 the Underwood Tariff Act reduced import duties that restricted international trade. The same year, the Federal Reserve Act changed the currency management system and established the 12 Federal Reserve Banks to add stability to the banking system. In 1914 the Clayton Antitrust Act and the establishment of the Federal

A portrait of Woodrow Wilson. After initially avowing neutrality he later felt he had no choice but to lead the United States into the war.

Trade Commission both curbed the powers of large corporations. The act outlawed business schemes used to create trust monopolies, while strengthening union rights, chiefly by prohibiting businesses from using legal injunctions against strikers, except in cases damaging to national security. It also legalized secondary boycotts that were used to back up original strike action. Among its wide-ranging powers the commission could issue cease-and-desist orders if trusts

A poster from 1915 shows Wilson offering humble pie as "a present from the U.S.A." to the hungry German eagle, referring to the United States' reluctance to enter the conflict.

were found to be performing outlawed trade practices.

In November 1914, when World War I had already been raging in Europe for three months, Wilson was sufficiently satisfied with his work to publish a public letter announcing that the legislative program of his first term was complete. Various groups were far from satisfied, however. Associations of women, industrial workers, socialists, farmers, and social reformers believed that more remained to be done to build a fair and equitable nation. Wilson had his mind on other problems, however, and further legislation was not forthcoming.

DOLLAR DIPLOMACY
The second key area of U.S. politics during the first years of World War I revolved around the country's maintenance of its

geopolitical and economic influence in its own backyard, chiefly Latin America and the Caribbean. Wilson essentially continued what was termed Dollar Diplomacy. This policy, which became prominent after 1900, advocated using diplomacy and direct military intervention by the government to promote U.S. business interests overseas. From 1914 to 1916 there were several examples of Dollar Diplomacy in action. Haiti, for example, which was beset by political turmoil, had consistently refused U.S. offers to establish a protectorate there. In 1915 marines landed to restore order, after which the government signed a trade agreement giving the United States control of its economy. Santo Domingo, also politically unstable and with an economy dominated by U.S. investment, was occupied by marines in 1916. They successfully ended an insurrection and placed the country under military rule for eight years. Elsewhere marines who had landed in 1912 to end a revolution continued to occupy Nicaragua and also maintained a strong presence in Honduras, where 80 percent of the vital banana industry was run by U.S. companies.

The greatest threat to Dollar Diplomacy during Wilson's first term came from Mexico, where some 80 percent of the railroads and 70 percent of the oil industry were under U.S. control. Some 40,000 American citizens lived in the country.

Previous U.S. presidents had been little interested in Mexico's internal politics so long as the ruling president was not hostile to U.S. business interests. Wilson took a stronger moral line. In 1913 a coup led to the assassination of the president, Francisco Madero,

and left the rebel leader, General Victoriano Huerta, in charge of the country. Wilson backed a rival to the presidency, Venustiano Carranza. After an incident involving Mexican troops U.S. Marines landed at the port of Veracruz and occupied it on July 14, 1914, to enforce respect for the U.S. flag. Meanwhile Huerta resigned, a victim of the Mexican Revolution, and the United States recognized Carranza as president in 1915.

PANCHO VILLA
U.S. involvement did not end with Carranza's assumption of the presidency. One of his former allies, the revolutionary and bandit leader Francisco "Pancho" Villa, turned on Carranza and on the United States because of its backing for the new president (see box). He halted a train carrying U.S. engineers bound for Chihuahua at Santa Isabel and murdered 15 of them, an act that provoked outrage in the United States. On March 9, 1916, Villa led 485 rebels across the border and attacked the town of Columbus, New Mexico, which held a garrison of the U.S. 13th Cavalry. After a gunfight Villa withdrew, leaving the town destroyed and 18 Americans dead. Demands for direct military intervention in Mexico grew.

As the U.S. garrisons along the Mexican border were strengthened, Wilson ordered General John J. Pershing (1860–1948) and 6,000 men to pursue Villa. The expedition crossed into Mexico on March 15, but Villa proved an elusive target in the bleak desert of northern Mexico, where he found support among villagers. The invasion also angered Carranza, who saw it as an affront to Mexican sovereignty. Clashes broke out between Mexican and

Pancho Villa

Pancho Villa (1877–1923) was born Doroteo Arango in the Mexican state of Durango. He changed his name to Francisco Villa but later became known as Pancho Villa as a bandit leader in his home state. Villa was a rebel general during the Mexican Revolution from 1910 to 1920, fighting for those who supported reform of the Mexican economy in favor of the country's large numbers of dispossessed peasants and native Indians. After the death of President Porfirio Díaz in 1911 Francisco Madero governed until his murder in 1913, when Victoriano Huerta took his place. Huerta distrusted Villa, who formed his own military band, called the Division of the North. When Venustiano Carranza rebelled against Huerta in 1914, Villa joined forces with him; once Carranza won power, however, the two men soon fell out and Villa turned against his ally.

At first Woodrow Wilson and the United States encouraged Villa. To achieve economic stability, however, Wilson decided to back Carranza after Carranza's chief general, Alvaro Obregón, defeated Villa at the Battle of Celaya in 1915. Villa, infuriated by the American turnaround, retaliated by stopping trains in Mexico and shooting Americans on board. In 1916 he led his men across the border to raid Columbus, New Mexico. They burned the town and killed 18 Americans.

This prompted Wilson to send 6,000 U.S. soldiers led by General John Pershing into Mexico with the objective of getting rid of Villa (below). Pershing, however, failed to capture the rebel, who knew the country well and had support from Mexico's peasants. Pershing's exploits served only to offend the Mexicans, including Carranza. They considered the expedition an attempt to interfere politically in Mexican affairs. Wilson called off the expedition in January 1917, having spent $130 million on failing to catch Villa.

Later, in 1920 Obregón turned against Carranza and had him killed. He offered Villa a grant of land. Villa accepted the offer and retired to a ranch there. Villa's support of land reform and his role in revolution had made him a champion of many ordinary Mexicans, though a criminal in the eyes of others, including the United States. He was ambushed and killed by his enemies in 1923.

Votes for Women

As in other countries, the contributions of women to the war effort in the United States strongly supported their campaign for the right to vote. The campaign had begun in the mid-19th century. In 1890 two suffrage organizations combined to form the National American Woman Suffrage Association.

Various states, led by Wyoming, gave women the right to vote, and by 1918 women had equal suffrage to men in 15 states. The suffragists made concerted efforts to recruit socially and politically prominent supporters. The Progressive movement grew in popularity, and many of its leaders supported woman suffrage. The war had broken down much opposition to female suffrage, which had been promoted by increasingly radical suffragists, such as Alice Paul (1885–1977). Paul led a band of pickets outside the White House each day, protesting the fact that while America was fighting for democracy, it would not let its own female citizens vote. Paul and her supporters were attacked by passersby; she served three terms in prison.

By 1918 both major parties supported female suffrage. NAWSA president Carrie Chapman Catt (1859–1947) launched a vigorous campaign to lobby Wilson for his support. In 1918 and 1919 Congress and the Senate passed the Nineteenth Amendment giving women the vote. The act became law in 1920.

A women's suffrage headquarters in Cleveland, Ohio, in 1912. Women had long campaigned for the vote before their contribution to the war effort and their role in the workforce added weight to their case.

The scenes U.S. politicians tried to avoid: American troops on the Western Front in Europe, 1918.

on the provisions of the Declaration of London (1906). On August 6, 1914, Wilson's counsellor at the State Department, Robert Lansing (1864–1928), asked the various belligerents to stand by the declaration's provisions with regard to neutral vessels. He later insisted that U.S. companies should be allowed to sell goods to any of the warring nations.

The British, however, interpreted the declaration differently

U.S. troops, chiefly at Carrizal on June 21. This inconclusive battle increased pressure on Wilson as his political rivals and some commentators argued for full-scale war. Wilson was more circumspect. He wanted to preserve the small U.S. Army intact as a basis for a much larger force if, as seemed increasingly likely, the United States had to intervene in World War I. In January 1917 Pershing left Mexico without finding the bandit.

2. AMERICA MOVES TOWARD WAR

Although U.S. government policy between 1914 and 1916 was in some respects "business as usual," World War I increasingly impinged on the administration's international and domestic policies. There were three main reasons for this. First, the United States was an international trading nation, and much of its trade was with the European nations now at war with each other. Second, Wilson, an idealist, believed that the United States was above the

rivalries that had led to World War I and therefore could and should act as a fair and independent mediator to bring about an end to the fighting. Third, U.S. society contained significant minorities, many recent immigrants who retained attachments to their countries of origin, which were now at war with each other. They organized groups that supported both sides in the war.

INTERNATIONAL TRADE

Trade was a key concern of the government, its opponents, and America's businesses and financial institutions. How could "strict neutrality" be adhered to when the country was trading widely with Europe, often providing goods that could be used in the war efforts of the combatants?

To some extent the question was answered by the combatants, chiefly Britain and Germany, both of which attempted to cut off their enemy's seaborne trade. At the outbreak of war Britain declared a naval blockade of Germany, based

Funding the Allies

Neutrality or not, Wilson came under pressure from leading U.S. bankers. They objected to proposals to prevent them from offering large loans overseas, which could be used to finance various war efforts and thus violated the principle of neutrality. The financiers argued that the loans would likely be used to buy U.S. goods, to the benefit of the country's economy. If they were prohibited, the various combatants would obtain finance and purchases elsewhere, to the detriment of U.S. business. Wilson eventually agreed to a relaxation of the financial policy. This overwhelmingly benefited the Allies. For example, on November 26, 1915, $50 million of credit was extended to a number of British banks.

A cartoon from 1915 shows Uncle Sam threatening to throw German snakes overboard, a reference to the "unpatriotic" attitude of German Americans to the war in Europe.

and took its provisions to give it wide powers. Ships carrying U.S. goods were stopped, boarded, and some impounded. The administration issued regular protests, but the British assuaged U.S. opinion by offering financial compensation for the goods it seized. The British blockade was highly effective: U.S. trade with Germany fell by 90 percent between December 1914 and January 1915. The potential harm to the U.S. economy was partly compensated for by a 250 percent rise in trade with neutral Scandinavia and by expanded dealings with the Allies.

German Blockades

The German blockade of Britain also became an increasing problem for the United States.

The Germans employed submarines that could patrol undetected from the surface. In February 1915 Germany declared the waters around Britain a war zone and stated that any vessel would be sunk without warning, a direct contravention of the Declaration of London. Wilson responded by stating that the United States would adopt a policy of "strict accountability." In other words, if American lives were lost in such attacks, those responsible would be held wholly to blame. Wilson's resolve was soon to be tested. On March 15 the *Falaba*, a merchant ship, was sunk by a German

•

"Our actions in this crisis will determine the part we play when peace is made."

•

submarine. A U.S. citizen, Leon Thrasher, was among the dead. Worse was to follow. On May 1 the U.S. tanker *Gulflight* was sunk and two of its crew killed.

The *Lusitania* Sunk

On May 7, 1915, a German submarine sank the British liner *Lusitania* off the south coast of Ireland. Among the 1,000 or so passengers and crew killed were 128 Americans. The sinking of a

passenger vessel caused outrage in the United States, though later investigations supported the German claim that the ship was carrying arms to aid the Allies.

One of Wilson's advisers, Edward House, stated bluntly, "We can no longer remain neutral spectators. Our actions in this crisis will determine the part we play when peace is made." Wilson, however, believed he might be able to maintain U.S. honor without going to war. He still could not be sure that the American public would wholeheartedly accept entry into the conflict.

Wilson was also reluctant to encourage further divisions within American society. Americans such as former president Theodore Roosevelt railed against groups they perceived as disloyal, chiefly German-Americans, Irish-Americans, pacifist campaigners, and supposed war profiteers. Roosevelt denounced such groups as "the hyphenated Americans, the solid flub dub and pacifist vote."

Wilson Warns Germany

Wilson responded to the sinking of the *Lusitania* by issuing increasingly stern warnings to Germany. The first, demanding a full explanation and apology, was sent on May 13. The German response was dismissed as inadequate. The second diplomatic note, from June 9, was blunt: Germany had to end unrestricted submarine warfare, and there could be no compromise on the issue. The note prompted Secretary of State William Jennings Bryan, a pacifist, to resign. He correctly believed that Germany was unlikely to end the submarine campaign permanently and that the United States would in all likelihood be dragged into the conflict. A third warning note was issued on July 21.

Secretary of State W. J. Bryan resigned in protest against what he saw as the inevitability of war.

A cartoon from World War I shows belligerents laughing at a poster that portrays Woodrow Wilson as Don Quixote on a donkey.

Submarine Warfare

In the summer of 1915 German submarine attacks continued. On August 19 the *Arabic*, a passenger liner, was sunk with the loss of three U.S. lives. The president's response to the loss was forthright and left little room for compromise: The submarine campaign had to end immediately, or the United States would react forcefully. The message had the desired effect. Germany announced that its submarines would henceforth avoid such attacks on passenger ships and that it would abandon the waters around Great Britain.

This suspension was short-lived. The German military leadership was soon persuading its government that a return to unrestricted conflict would lead to the rapid defeat of Britain. In March 1916 the military prevailed, and submarines returned to certain waters off Britain, although they were still forbidden to attack passenger ships. Just a few days later, on March 24, a passenger ferry, the *Sussex*, was sunk in the English Channel, and three Americans died. Wilson immediately threatened that the United States would break off diplomatic relations with Germany if the submarine attacks continued. The announcement was one step away from a war declaration, and Germany again backed down.

On April 24 its submarine captains were ordered not to attack neutral vessels without warning. Wilson's diplomacy, which extracted this "*Sussex* pledge" from Germany, appeared to have had the desired effect.

THE 1916 ELECTION

Wilson and his supporters made political capital out of the *Sussex* pledge in the 1916 presidential election. His supporters could argue that the pledge showed that Wilson was dedicated to maintaining U.S. neutrality through a policy of strong action. The president campaigned under the banner "He Kept Us Out of the War." One speaker at the Democratic Party convention observed that U.S. international rights had been upheld "without orphaning a single American child, without widowing a single American mother." However, Wilson's race to be reelected against Republican Charles Evans Hughes was close. In November he gained 277 votes in the electoral college, while Hughes received 254 votes.

THE SEARCH FOR PEACE

At the outbreak of World War I Colonel Edward House had reported from Europe that the conflict was a product of "militarism gone mad." Wilson, a high-minded figure, believed that the secretive manner in which Europe's world powers had conducted their international affairs,

Pro-German Americans

In August 1914 some German-Americans moved to offset the wealth of pro-Allied propaganda in the United States. In New York, for example, the German-American Literary Defense Committee distributed more than 50,000 pro-German tracts between August and December 1914. A German-American newspaper, George Sylvester Viereck's *The Fatherland*, was launched on August 10 and reached a circulation of 100,000 by October. There were also fund-raising exercises, such as one at St. Louis, Mo., which raised $20,000 for war relief. Other German-Americans, often acting alone, offered more active— and violent—support for Germany. On June 2, 1915, the pro-British U.S. banker John Pierpoint Morgan, Jr., survived an assassination attempt by a German Cornell University tutor in a Senate reception room. There were also incidents of German sabotage attacks on railroads and on industries.

as well as their political rivalries in the past, had brought about the war. He also continued to believe that the United States could very well act as an even-handed mediator that could, in time, bring about an end to the hostilities.

Wilson first extended peace-feelers in 1914 but met with little positive reaction. Matters seemingly improved, but it soon became apparent that neither the Allies nor the Central Powers were willing to contemplate a peace settlement without gaining some advantage. Both sides believed they could still win the war.

Failure of Diplomacy

Further efforts followed in late 1916. On December 18, after a somewhat ambiguous German effort to initiate talks, Wilson publicly demanded that the warring factions disclose the terms on which they would be willing to discuss a peace settlement. He also secretly contacted both Britain and Germany, offering to chair any subsequent negotiations. Wilson's December "Peace Note" was ill-received. The response was best summed up by Britain's war leader, David Lloyd George: "We accepted this war for an object [the defeat of the Central Powers], a worthy object, and the war will end when that objective is attained. Under God I hope it will never end until that time." Such sentiments marked the failure of Wilson's high-minded diplomacy. He had been constant in his desires for peace between 1914 and 1916, but failed to recognize the scale of the long-established animosities that divided the Allies and the Central Powers.

3. WAR AND THE AMERICAN PEOPLE

Between 1914 and 1917 Americans had to deal with the domestic and international fallout of the war. Some powerful individuals lamented what they saw as Wilson's weakness and his inability either to limit the effect of the war on the country or to preserve U.S. honor by standing up for the nation. Chief among

such critics was Theodore Roosevelt, who wanted the country to take a more decisive role in international events. Roosevelt argued for the creation of a draft system to facilitate military training. He was supported by former senior members of the armed forces, like ex-U.S. Army chief of staff General Leonard Wood (1860–1927), and bodies such as the National Security League.

These various groups, collectively known as the Preparedness Movement, were supported by some leading entrepreneurs, including Cornelius Vanderbilt and

•

"We accepted this war for an object...and [it] will end when that objective is attained."

•

Simon Guggenheim. Backing also came from the leader of the American Federation of Labor, Samuel Gompers. Labor was benefiting from higher wages due to the growing expansion of overseas trade brought about by the Allied demand for war goods; tough government action would ensure the boom continued. On August 10, 1915, the first training camp sponsored by the Preparedness Movement opened at Plattsburg, New York, and others followed. By the summer of 1916 some 16,000 Americans were attending "Plattsburg Camps."

PREPARING FOR WAR

By this stage of the war Wilson himself was making moves to prepare the United States and its people for a possible future role in the war. In December 1915 the National Defense Act authorized the doubling of the U.S. Army and the strengthening of the National Guard over a five-year period. The following year the Naval Appropriations Act called for a large program of warship construction. The strength of the U.S. Navy, already the world's third largest fleet in 1914, was to be increased by, among other warships, 16 battleships and battle cruisers.

Unlike members of the Preparedness Movement, most ordinary Americans were little concerned with the war, although the greater majority were broadly sympathetic to the Allied cause, viewing the Central Powers, chiefly Germany, as the instigators of the war. However, there were noteworthy exceptions. Among a total U.S. population of some 95 million sizable minorities were recent immigrants from Germany and Austria-Hungary. German-Americans accounted for some 8.5 percent of the population and Austro-Hungarians some 2.5 percent. Both groups lived in small, tight-knit communities that maintained links with their countries of origin and had developed pressure groups to protect their interests before the war. For example, some two million German-Americans were believed to be members of the National German-American Central Alliance, a body created at the turn of the century to protect the community against the reforming efforts of organizations such as the Prohibitionist Anti-Saloon League. The alliance was supported by wealthy major brewing interests, most of which had German origins.

Another group of recent immigrants to the United States was also eager to minimize U.S. support for the Allies. Irish Americans, some 5 percent of the country's population, had little

President Wilson makes his speech announcing entry into the war before Congress in 1917.

A poster advertising the National League for Women's Service. Miss America reports for duty.

desire to support Britain, which they saw as a colonial power occupying their old homeland.

A significant minority of American citizens were wholly opposed not just to U.S. participation in the conflict but to war in general. The Socialist Party, which had reached its high-water mark in the election of 1912, opposed the war. On August 29, 1914, social reformer Fanny Garrison Villard led 1,500 women through New York to protest for peace. Many of the various antiwar groups that emerged had a broader political agenda, chiefly relating to social reform, not least the emancipation of women.

4. THE MOVE TO WAR

The spring of 1917 saw the United States move decisively from peace to war chiefly because of Germany's continued maritime campaign against Britain. Despite the *Sussex* Pledge of the previous year, its leadership gave up hopes of a favorable peace settlement at the end of 1916, when the Allies rejected a half-hearted German proposal for talks to end the fighting. The Germans gambled that an unrestricted submarine campaign—sinking vessels without warning—would bring Britain to its knees in weeks. This was risky since further sinkings of any U.S. shipping were likely to push Wilson into a war declaration. The United States severed diplomatic relations with Germany on February 3 and on March 13 announced that all U.S. merchant ships were to be armed.

RELATIONS WITH GERMANY COLLAPSE

U.S.-German relations deteriorated even more in March. The British had intercepted a message between the German foreign

A crowd gathers to watch a lynching. Although such events were relatively rare, supposed traitors—often African Americans—received harsh treatment from "patriots."

minister, Arthur Zimmermann, and his ambassador to Mexico, deliberately designed to provoke the United States into war with Mexico and Japan. The telegram, passed to Wilson by way of his ambassador in Britain, Walter Hines Page, suggested that Mexico should enter into a defensive alliance with Germany whereby German submarines would be permitted to use Mexican ports, and Mexico was to "reconquer the lost territory in New Mexico, Texas, and Arizona," which had been part of Mexico until the mid-19th century. A further suggestion was that Mexico should encourage Japan, one of the Allied powers but a major rival to the United States in the Pacific, to join the Central Powers. The Zimmermann Telegram was made public in the United States on March 1 and proceeded to cause widespread outrage across the country.

DECLARATION OF WAR

U.S. shipping losses to German submarines continued to rise throughout the spring of 1917, culminating between March 16 and 18 with the loss of three vessels—*City of Memphis*, *Illinois*, and *Vigilancia*—with considerable loss of life. Two days later Wilson met with his cabinet to discuss the recent events. Those present were unanimous and mandated the president to ask Congress to support a declaration of war. The message was delivered on April 2, and war was declared against Germany on April 6. A similar declaration against Austria-Hungary was made on December 7.

"ASSOCIATED POWER"

The key problem facing Wilson's administration in April 1917 was how to transform the United States into a nation capable of fighting a large-scale war overseas yet avoid being identified too closely with the war aims of Britain and France. The United States insisted that it be known as an "associated power" rather than an ally, a committed but independent member of the Allied cause. All of the country's major institutions—social, economic, and military—would have to be changed to a lesser or greater degree to support the war effort.

The U.S. Expeditionary Force

One of the chief contributions the United States made to World War I was manpower. The regular army was made up of only 128,000 men when the country first entered the war. To build up the numbers, a draft was put in place that required all men from 21 to 30 years of age to register for military service. By 1918, however, that age range had been increased to between 18 and 45 years of age. A lottery determined who would actually serve in the army, although many men enlisted as volunteers. Women signed up as nurses and office workers. By the end of the war the U.S. Army comprised about five million men and women, out of which 2.75 million had been drafted.

Few U.S. soldiers had time to receive proper training before going overseas because they were so urgently required by the Allies. The U.S. soldiers formed what was called the American Expeditionary Force (AEF). General John J. Pershing, commander of the AEF, arrived in France in mid-June 1917. The first U.S. troops, who became known as "Doughboys," landed later that month (below). The Allies wanted Americans to serve as replacements for their own troops so as to fill out their battered ranks. But Pershing was convinced that the AEF would make a greater contribution by fighting as an independent formation and held firm on this point.

Wilson would also have to win the support of the country's citizens for the distant war.

Public Support

Wilson chose to garner public support for the war through a mixture of persuasion and coercion. On April 13, 1917, journalist George Creel (1876–1953) was placed in charge of the newly founded Committee on Public Information. His brief was to convince the U.S. people of the war's necessity and justice. Aside from managing the press, the committee released movies and

Personal Decisions

Some Americans made highly personal decisions regarding World War I. Many traveled to Europe, where they established or joined bodies to ameliorate the human suffering brought about by the conflict. Overwhelmingly they operated on the Allied side of the lines. Novelist Edith Wharton, for example, established the American Hostels for Refugees in Paris during November 1914, while many younger Americans, often students at Ivy League universities, formed ambulance corps in France to look after the war's military wounded. Writer Ernest Hemingway drove an ambulance on the Italian front. Other citizens joined up to fight for the Allies, including poet Alan Seegar, who was to lose his life in the Battle of the Somme in 1916.

posters, and some 75 million pamphlets. Around 75,000 public speakers, called the "Four-Minute Men" for the speed with which they put their message across, toured the country to boost support for the war.

The campaign whipped up emotion against some of the immigrant community. It led some states to prohibit church services in German and to excise German terms from public use. Sauerkraut became "liberty cabbage," for example, and the dachshund was renamed the "liberty dog." Various organizations developed—many semiofficial bodies like the National Security League—to seek out and expose traitors and "slackers." There were also more pernicious examples of local vigilantism against German-Americans, even though many of them had joined loyalty leagues to demonstrate their support of their new country. Numerous German newspapers and community institutions were forced to close; many never reopened.

Other political groups also made capital out of the national mood for promoting a "pure" form of Americanism based on loyalty and patriotism. In the summer of 1917 Prohibitionists engineered an amendment to new legislation that

U.S. troops on the Western Front keep watch from an improvised front-line trench during the Allied advance in October 1918.

pursued "purity" by forbidding the use of foodstuffs in the manufacture of distilled liquor. This led the way for full-scale Prohibition (see Chapter 3, "The Return to Normalcy"). Prohibitionists also gained support because of the traditional association of beer and brewing with German-Americans.

Enemies Within

The administration also used catch-all legislation to combat supposed "enemies within." Various acts addressed those Americans seen as opposing the war efforts, chiefly antiwar protesters, political radicals, conscientious objectors, African American activists, and recent immigrants. The Espionage Act of June 15, 1917, for example, allowed fines of up to $10,000 and prison terms of up to 20 years for individuals obstructing the war effort by spying, sabotage, interfering with recruitment, encouraging military insubordination, and refusing to serve in the military. The postmaster was authorized to stop delivery of subversive material in the U.S. mail. Immediately after the war such legislation would play an important part in the anticommunist "Red Scare" (see box, page 41).

THE U.S. ECONOMY AT WAR

In late spring 1917 it was clear that a wide-ranging reform of the country's financial and economic structures was necessary to support the war. The financing of the war was regularized by a series of War Revenue acts, the

This photograph from 1918 shows troops facing a gas attack. It was probably used to encourage U.S. troops to wear their gas masks.

provisions of which were masterminded by Secretary of the Treasury William Gibbs McAdoo (1863–1941). Government income was to be increased through two mechanisms. First, taxes were to be raised on incomes and through excise duties. These measures provided some 50 percent of new revenue. Second, a total of some $23 billion was borrowed from two sources: the public sale of war bonds, popularly known as "Liberty Bonds," and the exchange of such bonds for financial credits from major banks. Liberty Bonds were promoted through the media, by rallies, and through tours of sporting and entertainment celebrities. They proved highly popular, raising some $17 billion.

Wilson's administration also had to reorganize the mechanisms

A poster showing "Liberty" calling for the billions of dollars needed to support the war.

and institutions that directed the country's economy, chiefly by removing the inefficiencies caused by competition, cutting back on nonessential production, reducing

APREMONT, FRONT LINE TOWN OF THE GERMANS IN THE ST MIHIEL

waste, and tackling unrestrained public consumption.

Initially, production failed to keep pace with the nation's war needs. In 1917 the War Industries Board was created to allocate resources and to fix output and prices for manufacturers and boards established to urge Americans to conserve fuel and food. Congress passed the Overman Act in May 1918, which granted the president significant powers to manage the economy. Wilson delegated many of these powers to boards or commissions that reported directly to him.

Overseeing all these bodies was the Council of National Defense, established by the Military Appropriations Act of 1916. The Council included cabinet officials, such as Secretary of War Newton Baker, and other special advisers. Beneath the Council of National Defense lay the organizations responsible for one or another sector of the economy, including the War Industries Board, headed by businessman Bernard Baruch. Other bodies also increased federal authority over the running of the economy. The Shipping Board, for instance, took control of the merchant fleet and oversaw a vast building program to replace vessels lost to enemy submarines, while the Railroad Administration placed the rail system under central authority and paid rent to

the private owners for its use. Other bodies included the War Trades Board, the War Finance Corporation, and the War Labor Policies Board. Future president Herbert Hoover was given charge of the Food Administration, which fixed prices, regulated production and distribution, and encouraged voluntary rationing through public drives, including "Wheatless Mondays" and "Porkless Thursdays." The federal involvement in the U.S. economy was unprecedented and anticipated the degree of involvement that would come in the early years of the Great Depression.

Sedition Act

In May 1917 the Espionage Act was strengthened by the Sedition Act. It listed offenses said to undermine the war effort and was mainly used against political radicals and labor activists. Among those convicted were Victor Berger, a founder of the Socialist Party of America, as well as Eugene V. Debs, the party's leader and 1912 presidential candidate, and William Haywood of the Industrial Workers of the World, a radical labor organization.

Apremont in the St. Mihiel, a frontline town captured by U.S. troops from the Germans in their offensive of 1918.

By early 1918 the effectiveness of the various bodies was beyond question. By June, for example, U.S. yards were launching four ships per day, and warships were being built in three to five months each. Food exports to the Allies were so great that around 44 percent of all Britons, 14 percent of the French, and 11 percent of Italians were surviving on U.S.-produced food. Britain received some $33 billion worth of goods, while the figure for France was a little over $2 billion.

Army Recruitment

Like the economy, the U.S. Army was initially ill-prepared for war. The regular U.S. Army, despite the National Defense Act, still comprised little more than 128,000 troops. It was supported by the Overseas Service on July 3, 1917, but together the two forces were still far too small to have any effect on the war. However, Wilson was already moving to vastly expand U.S. armed forces. Despite some opposition, the Selective Service Act was introduced on May 18. It allowed for conscription and gave the president the power to draft eligible citizens (see box, page 33). The first draft was announced in September, and some 517,000 men had been inducted by the year's end, along with 230,000 volunteers. Many more would follow.

U.S. Forces in Action

The first of the two million U.S. forces who eventually served in Europe saw action in the spring of 1918, when Germany launched an all-or-nothing series of offensives on the Western Front in France, which had been largely static throughout the four years of the war. U.S. units battled successfully at Cantigny, Chateau-Thierry, and Belleau Wood. These were relatively small-scale actions, but psychologically they had an important effect on the conflict. The Allies were boosted by the combat debut of Pershing's men, while Germany saw their presence at the front as a harbinger of growing U.S. commitment to the war and eventual German defeat.

Victorious U.S. troops crowd the deck of their ship as it docks at Hoboken, N.J., in 1919, after the voyage home across the Atlantic.

German fears were well founded. On September 11 some 500,000 U.S. troops attacked the German-held salient at St. Mihiel near Verdun and achieved their objectives in five days. As German morale collapsed in the final weeks of the war, Pershing led his forces in the largest U.S. offensive yet seen, an attack in the Meuse and Argonne. The advance began on September 26 and continued until the Armistice of November 11, 1918. Despite fierce German resistance, Pershing secured virtually all of his objectives. The U.S. Army suffered some 264,000 casualties during its brief period on the Western Front, of which more than 50,000 had been killed in action and 25,000 had succumbed to disease.

WILSON'S SEARCH FOR PEACE

In early 1918 it was clear that an Allied victory was the likely outcome of the war. Wilson determined that the United States should have a large say in any peace settlement. His chief concern was to make the world safe from future wars by ensuring

that the causes of conflict were eradicated. He wished to create a new political framework that would transform the nature of nations and the relationships between them. Wilson outlined his views to Congress on January 18, 1918, in a plan termed the Fourteen Points, which later formed the basis on which Austria-Hungary and Germany agreed to armistices with the Allies (see box, page 38).

Final Compromise

The Fourteen Points were ambitious; and although Wilson worked tirelessly to achieve them, he was thwarted by his fellow Allies. Wilson, so dedicated to establishing the League of Nations, compromised on virtually every other section of his plan during the peace discussions that followed the opening of the Treaty of Versailles in January 1919. It is perhaps ironic that Wilson's moral authority had led a reluctant country into war in 1917 and had in great part created the institutions that allowed it to play a large role in victory, yet the president was finally unable to impose his moral view on either his Allies or his own people (see Chapter 3, "The Return to Normalcy").

——— SEE ALSO ———

◆ Volume 1, Chapter 1, The United States, 1865–1914

◆ Volume 1, Chapter 3, The Return to Normalcy

◆ Volume 1, Chapter 4, The Roaring Twenties

◆ Volume 6, Chapter 5, The United States in World War II

THE RETURN TO NORMALCY

With the war over, the American people were impatient to return to a way of life they considered normal. It was time once again to get down to the business of business, to increase output, expand distribution, and create profits. But America was wary and uneasy about events in Europe and at home.

The war in western Europe ended with the Armistice of November 11, 1918 (see Chapter 2, "The United States in World War I"). The end of the conflict, however, did not mean the end of U.S. involvement in Europe. President Woodrow Wilson, who in January 1918 had proposed his Fourteen Points as the basis of a peace settlement (see box), was determined that the United States should play a prominent role in the Paris Peace Conference of 1919.

1. THE END OF THE WAR

In Europe Wilson was praised for the American contribution to the conflict and the morality of his peace aims. When he landed in France and drove through the streets of Paris, he was hailed by the French as "Wilson le Juste."

The mood of Americans at home was different. Many were more interested in returning their attention to American concerns. Wilson's own political position was weakening, partly because he entirely left the Republicans out of the peace process. He returned home to find opposition to the

The Fourteen Points

Woodrow Wilson's Fourteen Points were declared in January 1918 and were the basis of his desire for a "peace without victories."
1. Open diplomacy; no secret treaty making
2. Freedom of the seas in war as well as in peace
3. The removal of all economic barriers to international trade
4. National armaments to be reduced
5. Colonial disputes to be judged impartially, with equal weight being given to the interests of the subject populations and the claims of the colonial governments
6. The evacuation by the Germans and Austrians of all Russian territory
7. The restoration of Belgian sovereignty
8. All occupied French territory to be restored and Alsace and Lorraine to be returned to France
9. Italy's frontiers to be readjusted along clearly recognized lines of nationality
10. The peoples of Austria-Hungary to be given the opportunity for autonomous development
11. Romania, Serbia, and Montenegro to be restored and Serbia given access to the sea, and Balkan interstate relations to be settled on lines of allegiance and nationality
12. The non-Turkish peoples of the Ottoman Empire to be given the opportunity for autonomous development
13. The establishment of a Polish state with access to the sea
14. A general association of nations to be formed to guarantee political independence and territorial integrity to great and small states alike

Returning U.S. servicemen are reunited with their families after the end of World War I.

peace treaties and the League of Nations growing in Congress.

Reaction to the treaty was split into three groups. The first, Wilson and his supporters, argued that the treaty should be ratified without any major changes. The second group, the isolationists, argued that America should not be involved in European affairs. They were led by senators William E. Borah, Hiram W. Johnson, and James A. Reed. The third and largest group, led by Henry Cabot Lodge (1850–1924), took the middle ground and argued for ratification with major changes that would greatly reduce America's obligations in Europe. In the end, however, America opted for isolationism.

WILSON'S DEFEAT

Although the United States had emerged from the war relatively unscathed, many Americans felt an intense revulsion about a conflict that had cost more than 10 million lives. They believed that the United States should now leave Europe to rebuild itself rather than risk becoming involved in future conflicts. Some people argued that Europe needed help to reschedule debts, to build up its industrial base, and to re-establish peacetime political regimes, but the United States was not interested in giving aid.

The Senate rejected the Versailles Peace Treaty because Article 10 bound signatories to come to the aid of member states if they were attacked. Neither would the United States join the League of Nations set up to oversee what

Wilson grandly referred to as a "just peace."

In order to attract support from the American people, Wilson planned a speaking tour to explain his vision of the future. The tour taxed his physical and mental health: He suffered permanent headaches. On September 22, 1919, he made a moving speech in Pueblo, Colorado, invoking the American soldiers who had died during the war, then broke down in tears. He quit the tour and returned to Washington, D.C., where he suffered a stroke on October 2. For the next 17 months the president was rarely well enough to take part in government, although his wife, Edith, relayed his wishes to members of the administration.

While the United States still debated its participation, Wilson's dream, the League of Nations, was inaugurated on January 16, 1920. The founding nations—which included France, Great Britain, Italy, and Japan—declared that a seat would be kept vacant for America. Wilson won the Nobel Peace Prize for his efforts to bring a "lasting settlement of the issues that led to the Great War."

2. THE CHANGE TO "NORMALCY"

The American people, in any case, wanted change. Many were tired of the president's high-minded preaching and moralizing. They were ready to return to "normal" politics, meaning Republicanism, which had dominated the United States since the Civil War. Wilson had been elected in 1912 only because Theodore Roosevelt split the Republican vote. The economic situation also drew support away from Wilson. During the last few months of his presidency the government ended the tight

A poster calls on people to protect democracy from communism, symbolized by a hammer and sickle.

financial regulations that had been in force during the war. It cut back on spending while allowing prices to double as government controls relaxed. Unemployment increased, and strikes became more common. The apparently unsympathetic attitude of the government reduced its support.

Even before the war there had been concern about the growing presence of anarchists and socialists. The speed at which the effects of the 1917 Bolshevik revolution in Russia spread around the world alarmed Americans. The formation in 1919 of the Third International, dedicated to spreading communism worldwide, was more alarming still. There were communist risings in the German region of Bavaria and in Hungary. Rumors circulated that funds had been sent to New York to pay for subversives to spread Bolshevik communism—

"bolshevism"—in the United States.

The Bolsheviks believed that America was ripe for revolution. Their sympathizers infiltrated the foreign language factions of the American Socialist Party and after 1919 the newly formed American Communist Party. Only 7 percent of the members spoke or understood English. The communists organized labor unions for militant action. There were strikes every month. In 1919 a total of about four million workers went on strike in various disputes. A strike of Seattle shipworkers precipitated a general walkout that brought the town to a complete standstill. Such a situation served to alienate the middle classes and seemed to many to illustrate just how close a revolution might be. Their fears were further confirmed when a series of parcel bombs was delivered to senators and other figures of authority around the country. Eight cities suffered coordinated bomb attacks for which communists, who may or may not have been responsible, got the blame.

COMMUNIST INVASION AND RED RIOTS

In 1919 three major strikes hit the United States: by the police in Boston, and by the nation's steel workers and coal miners. The workers had genuine grievances: They worked long hours with low pay and could not afford increasing food prices. Many of the strike leaders were conservative

unionists, but such was the mood of the country that the disputes were blamed on radical groups. Middle America was convinced that the country was facing an invasion of alien revolutionaries. In 1919, while Wilson lay incapacitated in the White House, Attorney General A. Mitchell Palmer (1872–1936) launched his Red Scare (see box, opposite).

THE ELECTION OF 1920

As the election of 1920 approached, the Republicans were confident of victory. On a hot June day in 1920 a group of party bosses got together in what became famous as a "smoke-filled room" in the Blackstone Hotel, Chicago, to decide which of the three shortlisted candidates should be nominated. The leading contender was General Leonard Wood (1860–1927), a hero of the war in Cuba; second and third were Governor Frank Lowden of Illinois and Senator Hiram Johnson. In the early hours of the next morning, however, the party selected the fourth choice, a loyal but largely inactive senator from Ohio, Warren Gamaliel Harding (1865–1923). Although rumors persisted that Harding's nomination had been fixed by business interests, it remains uncertain that that was so. Many of the senators at the meeting continued to try to block Harding's nomination next day at the convention, contradicting the theory that a deal had been done to secure his victory. Eventually, however, he was nominated on the 10th ballot.

THE ELECTION CAMPAIGN

Harding was a handsome, easygoing newspaper publisher and senator with no particular skills to suit him for the role of president. One Republican warned against

The Red Scare

Government reaction to the threat of communism in the years immediately following the Russian Revolution in 1917 and the end of the war a year later reached its peak in 1919, when Attorney General A. Mitchell Palmer started a campaign against America's "enemies."

There were legitimate worries behind Palmer's fears. Europe was in a state of political upheaval. Four million Americans went on strike through the year; race riots broke out in many cities and towns; some 70 black Americans were lynched in 1919 alone. Anarchists and radicals in the United States planted bombs and distributed leaflets against the American system.

Palmer, who previously had a reputation as being sympathetic toward immigrants, changed his approach when his own home was bombed. He set up an antiradical division in the Department of Justice under J. Edgar Hoover— the division later became the FBI. Between November 1919 and February 1920 Palmer and Hoover deported between 5,000 and 10,000 "alien" members of radical parties on "red arks." Police entered meeting halls and homes looking for suspects. There was no proper legal process. Suspects were usually handcuffed, chained together, and marched through the streets. They were thrown into jail, often with no food.

Palmer announced that a revolution would begin on May 1, 1920, but nothing happened. By then numerous public figures had begun to protest against the Palmer-Hoover raids, which were happening on such a scale that injustices were inevitable. Louis Post, who was acting secretary of labor, investigated many individual cases and could find little basis for many of the arrests. He approved only 556 deportations of the thousands that took place and was backed when America's leading lawyers also condemned the Department of Justice. After the May Day revolution failed to happen, the Palmer-Hoover raids ceased.

Attorney General A. Mitchell Palmer began his political career as a progressive reformer but later deported hundreds of people for their political beliefs.

Harding rides with his predecessor, Woodrow Wilson, to his inaugural in 1921; he was the first president to make the journey by motor car.

letting him spoil the presidential campaign: "Keep Warren at home," he warned. "Don't let him make any speeches. If he goes out on a tour somebody's sure to ask him questions, and Warren's just the sort of damned fool that will try to answer them."

In fact, the campaign went well. Harding proved effective in his call for what he dubbed "normalcy," the restoration of an older America. What the times required, he added, was "not heroism but healing, not nostrums but normalcy." The Democratic candidate, James Cox, failed to make an impact on Harding's popularity. The Republicans won the election—the first in which women could vote and the first whose results were broadcast by radio—with 60.3 percent of the popular vote, the highest share then known.

What Was Normalcy?

Harding's "front-porch" image as a commonsense Midwesterner appealed to Americans' nostalgia for the prewar years. It was easier to advocate "normalcy" than to define it, however, let alone produce it. The concept meant different things to different people. To some people it meant freedom and self-reliance; to others, it meant intolerance of radicals who criticized the American system, the prohibition of alcohol, or banning the teaching of evolution in public schools.

Harding's pursuit of normalcy led him to take a more practical approach to the peace settlement than the idealistic Wilson had adopted. He ended the deadlock over the Versailles peace treaties by signing a version that excluded the covenant that would have involved the United States in the League of Nations. In domestic legislation Congress placed quotas on immigration for the first time in 1921. It

Harding's Election

When Harding was elected as president in 1920, there was little doubt that he would win. The Democratic candidate, James Cox, governor of Ohio, his adversary's home state, had to fight an uphill battle. He and his party were hampered by their support for the unpopular Versailles Treaty and League of Nations, largely the creation of the outgoing president. The Democrats barely tried to overcome their disadvantages: They spent next to nothing on their campaign.

Harding started with a comfortable lead and kept it. At first the Republicans had decided to keep him to a "front porch" campaign, which meant he would be required to do little more than be seen and look the part. As it turned out, he proved an effective speaker, especially in his call for the country to return to how it used to be. It was the margin of victory that caused a stir, however. Harding won by a landslide, with 16.1 million votes to 9.1 million and 404 electoral votes to 127.

Reconstructing Harding

Harding's reputation has long been tarnished by allegations of corruption and incompetence. His wife aroused suspicion after his death by burning a number of big boxes of his papers. Today, however, some historians believe that Harding's poor reputation is not justified by events but was created by a series of biased attacks.

Criticism of Harding began as early as 1924 with a series of articles published in the *War Republic* by leftist editor Bruce Bliven. Bliven created the myth that the "Ohio Gang" run by Harry Daugherty—later Harding's attorney general and a politician most people still see as a crook—had deliberately recruited Harding as a frontman as part of a long-term conspiracy to hand over America to Andrew Mellon, the influential Pittsburgh banker who was secretary of the treasury under all three Republican presidents of the 1920s. There is no evidence for Bliven's charges.

Fiction also conspired to discredit Harding. The novel *Revelry* was about a president who poisoned himself to avoid scandals and exposure. When Hoover read it, he thought it was based on Harding. In *The President's Daughter* Nan Britton claimed to have given birth to the president's illegitimate daughter in 1919. She alleged that she had been seduced by Harding when he was a senator. Later evidence threw doubt on the claim that Harding was the baby's father.

Attacks on Harding continued with William Allen White's *Masks in a Pageant* and Gaston Means's *The Strange Death of President Harding*. The latter, which detailed drunken orgies with chorus girls at the "Little Green House" on K Street, is now dismissed as a collection of, at best, half-truths. *Crowded Hours*, by Alice Roosevelt Longworth, daughter of former president Theodore Roosevelt, presented Harding's White House as a "speakeasy." She described "...the air heavy with tobacco smoke, trays with bottles of every imaginable brand of whiskey stood about,

cards and poker chips ready at hand." Longworth concluded, "Harding was not a bad man. He was just a slob." Longworth was well known for her sharp tongue, however, and resented Harding's political success.

Finally, Samuel Hopkins Adams wrote *The Incredible Era: The Life and Times of Warren Gamaliel Harding*, in which he endorsed the myths that had already come to exist and added a few of his own. The book became the accepted history of Harding.

In 1964 scholars gained access to those Harding papers that had not been burned by the president's widow. They strongly suggested that Harding himself had been an honest president, if an undistinguished one. He accepted the fact that he was probably not up to the job. He once observed, "I am a man of limited talents from a small town. I don't seem to grasp that I am president." Part of his problem lay in the fact that he did not possess a true political philosophy. "Normalcy" was a broad idea that meant all things to all people. Harding did not have great political ambition, claiming, "I cannot hope to be one of the great presidents, but perhaps I may be remembered as one of the best loved." Harding allowed anybody to walk into the White House at lunchtime to meet him. During his term in office he met some 250,000 people in this way and claimed, "It is really the only fun I have."

Perhaps the main reason behind Harding's poor reputation was the people with whom he surrounded himself. Some of the friends to whom he gave government offices were naive or corrupt (see box, page 53) and scandals dogged Harding's term. When he died on August 2, 1923, while on a speaking tour in San Francisco, millions of citizens mourned his death. As details of the scandals became revealed over the following years, however, Harding's esteem fell. In 1931, at the dedication of Harding's Memorial Tomb, Herbert Hoover said that Harding had been "seared by a great disillusionment."

cut taxes the same year, and in 1922 the Fordney–McCumber Tariff raised import duties to record levels to protect U.S. businesses from foreign competition.

HARDING'S PERSONALITY

Harding's reputation has not always been good: He is often seen as too easygoing and indulgent, politically naive and open to charges of corruption. One of the president's failings, critics charge, was precisely that he was overly friendly and too willing to trust people who did not deserve it.

Such allegations mask the positive aspects of Harding's genuine liking for and sympathy with people. He restored blacks to the positions they had lost under Wilson. He actively tried to improve working conditions for labor. For instance, he helped end the 12-hour day at the blast furnaces of United States Steel. When the outspoken socialist leader Eugene V. Debs (1855–1926)—who had run for president from prison—

was released after serving a 32-month sentence, Harding made sure he was out of jail by Christmas because, he explained, "I want him to eat his Christmas dinner with his wife."

THE FAILURE OF ISOLATIONISM

Despite the desire for isolation from European affairs expressed by the refusal to join the League of Nations, the United States found itself inevitably drawn into international affairs. The nation's wealth, power, and business interests forced it to become involved, no matter how reluctantly, in the affairs of nearby Central America. American troops were active in Nicaragua, Haiti, Honduras, and Santo Domingo.

In the Pacific, too, U.S. trade interests saw Harding call an arms limitation conference of Pacific powers in Washington in 1921. He was concerned to limit Japan's power in the region, particularly in China. An "open door" agreement of 1917 had guaranteed all nations

Warren G. Harding (center) and his wife with Herbert Hoover (second from left) and Harry Daugherty (far right) at a baseball game in 1922.

equal rights to trade in China, but Japan's influence there was growing alarmingly. By the terms of the Washington Treaty of 1921 Japan agreed to limit the size of its navy: In fact, the treaty eventually helped consolidate the Japanese naval presence in the Pacific (see Volume 6, Chapter 1, "Economics and Political Extremism in Europe and Japan").

THE UNITED STATES AND EUROPE

The United States remained committed to staying outside European affairs as much as possible. Many Americans saw the political instability in Europe—like the rise to power in Italy in 1922 of the fascists of Benito Mussolini—as further evidence that America was better off outside Europe.

Winners and losers alike paid a heavy price to reconstruct Europe

A cartoon from 1922 shows Uncle Sam on a moneybag inside the United States listening to the message "No more isolation."

and to pay their war debts, mainly to the United States. In 1920 the Allies agreed to apportion payments for the war: France was to pay 52 percent, the British Empire 22 percent, Italy 10 percent, and Belgium 8 percent.

The following year the victors imposed reparations, or fines, on Germany totaling 200 million gold marks, or $35 billion. Germany complained that such a bill would cause "the economic and political pauperization of the German nation." The national trade union argued that America was trying to introduce slavery to the country. Some Germans called for an alliance with the Soviet Union against the Western powers.

Even Allied economists such as the Briton John Maynard Keynes (1883–1946) argued that such a heavy fine would prevent Germany from achieving economic recovery. Its inability to purchase goods would weaken the European economy as a whole and also undermine Germany's own ability to resist the spread of communism.

America and the Allies were determined to exact reparations, however, until hyperinflation in Germany in 1923 destroyed the currency and made it impossible for the Germans to pay. The Americans agreed to look again at the schedule of debts. Under the Dawes Plan of 1924 and later the 1929 Young Plan the United States acknowledged that it was economically damaging to remain separate

U.S. Marines search for bandits in Haiti in 1919. Isolationism did not prevent U.S. intervention in Latin America or the Pacific.

AN INSISTENT MESSAGE.

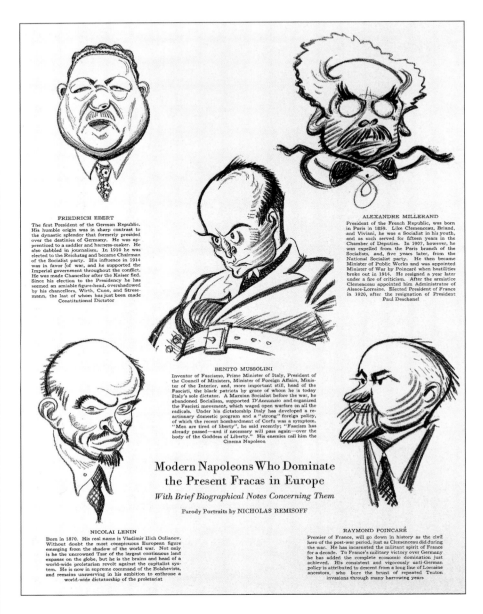

FRIEDRICH EBERT

The first President of the German Republic. His humble origin was in sharp contrast to the dynastic splendor that formerly presided over the destinies of Germany. He was apprenticed to a saddler and harness-maker. He also dabbled in journalism. In 1910 he was elected to the Reichstag and became Chairman of the Socialist party. His influence in 1914 was in favor [of] war, and he supported the Imperial government throughout the conflict. He was made Chancellor after the Kaiser fled. Since his election to the Presidency he has seemed an amiable figure-head, overshadowed by his chancellors, Wirth, Cuno, and Stresemann, the last of whom has just been made Constitutional Dictator

ALEXANDRE MILLERAND

President of the French Republic, was born in Paris in 1859. Like Clemenceau, Briand, and Viviani, he was a Socialist in his youth, and as such served for fifteen years in the Chamber of Deputies. In 1907, however, he was expelled from the Paris branch of the Socialists, and, five years later, from the National Socialist party. He then became Minister of Public Works and was appointed Minister of War by Poincaré when hostilities broke out in 1914. He resigned a year later under a fire of criticism. After the armistice Clemenceau appointed him Administrator of Alsace-Lorraine. Elected President of France in 1920, after the resignation of President Paul Deschanel

BENITO MUSSOLINI

Inventor of Fascismo, Prime Minister of Italy, President of the Council of Ministers, Minister of Foreign Affairs, Minister of the Interior, and, more important still, head of the Fascisti, the black patriots by grace of whom he is today Italy's sole dictator. A Marxian Socialist before the war, he abandoned Socialism, supported D'Annunzio and organized the Fascisti movement, which waged open warfare on all the radicals. Under his dictatorship Italy has developed a reactionary domestic program and a "strong" foreign policy, of which the recent bombardment of Corfu was a symptom. "Men are tired of liberty", he said recently; "Fascism has already passed—and if necessary will pass again—over the body of the Goddess of Liberty." His enemies call him the Cinema Napoleon

Modern Napoleons Who Dominate the Present Fracas in Europe

With Brief Biographical Notes Concerning Them

Parody Portraits by NICHOLAS REMISOFF

NICOLAI LENIN

Born in 1870. His real name is Vladimir Ilich Oulianov. Without doubt the most conspicuous European figure emerging from the shadow of the world war. Not only is he the uncrowned Tsar of the largest continuous land expanse on the globe, but he is the brains and head of a world-wide proletarian revolt against the capitalist system. He is now in supreme command of the Bolshevists, and remains unswerving in his ambition to enthrone a world-wide dictatorship of the proletariat

RAYMOND POINCARÉ

Premier of France, will go down in history as the civil hero of the post-war period, just as Clemenceau did during the war. He has incarnated the militant spirit of France for a decade. To France's military victory over Germany he has added the complete economic domination just achieved. His consistent and vigorously anti-German policy is attributed to descent from a long line of Lorraine ancestors, who bore the brunt of repeated Teuton invasions through many harrowing years

A cartoon gallery of Europe's troublemakers, including Mussolini (center) and Lenin (bottom left).

from European affairs. It stepped in to help stabilize the German currency. It loaned Germany money to pay to the Allies that they then sent to the United States in payment of their own debts.

Fascism in Italy

Germany's economic problems would eventually contribute to the rise of the extreme right-wing Nazi Party of Adolf Hitler. Americans could already see an example of the consequences of extremism in Italy. War debts and postwar reconstruction left Italy suffering high inflation, high prices, and low wages. Workers frequently went on strike in protest. Socialist revolution was in the air; many opponents of socialism joined the Fascist Party led by Benito Mussolini. In the winter of 1920 to 1921 the fascists began a campaign of violence against socialists. The government did little to stop the violence, but

rather welcomed it as a way of curbing troublesome socialists. The fascists' offer of stability and strength made them attractive to property-owners and the middle classes. In 1922 Mussolini came to power.

3. PROSPERITY AND UNEASE

In spite of the prosperity of postwar America, there was an underlying feeling of unease among the American people. They looked with distrust at elements in society that seemed ready to upset the equilibrium of their lives. At the same time, Americans were no longer sure that religion or democracy held the right answers after their experience of World War I.

INTERNAL THREATS

For many people the greatest threats to American stability came from within. Like Mitchell Palmer, many blamed America's unrest on immigrants. Around a million had entered the country every year between 1900 and the start of the war in 1914. As soon as war ended, the number of immigrants rose again. From June 1920 to June 1921 over 800,000 people entered the United States. The authorities could not cope, and Congress passed an emergency act to restrict immigration. The Emergency Quota Act had been passed the previous year but vetoed by Wilson; now Harding reenacted and signed it. It capped immigration from Europe at 357,000 per year but set no limits on arrivals from Canada or Latin America.

The National Origins Act

In 1924 Congress passed the National Origins Act, or Johnson-Reed Act, which established quotas of immigrants of different

Nicola Sacco (left) and Bartolomeo Vanzetti, secretly photographed in prison shortly before their execution in 1927.

ethnic origins. The act favored northern European settlers and completely barred all East Asian immigration under the provisions of the earlier Naturalization Act. The National Origins Act cut the total of immigrants in any one year to 164,000, with a final ceiling of 150,000 in 1927. Mass immigration had quickly become a thing of the past.

STEREOTYPING

Within the United States support for limiting immigration was reinforced by a frequent use of racial stereotyping. Most immigrant groups fell victim to crude stereotyping, especially the Italians, Germans, Poles, Mexicans, and to some extent the Scandinavians, as well as Russian Jews, Slavs, and southern Europeans generally. Black Americans also suffered from stereotyping. The Germans were portrayed as good natured but lazy, with a liking for beer. Italians were seen as slovenly and untrustworthy, while the Scandinavians, although part of the "Teutonic" race, were considered to be dour, with ice water running in their veins.

East Coast Highbrows

Not everyone saw America as a melting pot into which people from everywhere might be poured. Many intellectuals—often called the East Coast highbrows, a phrase invented by the critic Van Wyck Brooks—believed in a principle historian Henry Adams (1838–1918) had termed "multiversity." Adams suggested that Americans should look to a more cosmopolitan society to create the first "international nation," which would become more European in outlook but remain more adventurous than Europe itself. Adams intended this multiverse society to be led by the highbrows. When one of his friends, Waldo Frank, planned to settle in the Midwest, Adams wrote him: "All our will to live as writers comes to us, or rather stays with us, through our intercourse with Europe. Never believe people who talk to you about the West, Waldo; never forget that it is we New Yorkers and New Englanders who have the monopoly of whatever oxygen there is in the American continent." The concept of East Coast superiority continued to pervade

Sacco and Vanzetti

In 1920 two men were arrested and accused of a holdup and murder at a shoe factory in Massachusetts. Nicola Sacco and Bartolomeo Vanzetti were tried, found guilty, and sentenced to death. They spent seven years in jail while appeals were heard and more arguments made. The court was far more influenced by the fact that the accused were of Italian origin and had anarchist tendencies than by the evidence in the case. It is quite likely that the two did commit the crime of which they were accused, but the case seemed to make a nonsense of freedom and justice. It was more an act of class vengeance and anti-immigrant hysteria than of legal correctness. As the day of execution approached, there were strikes, riots, and marches in protest. But eventually the last appeal was denied, and Sacco and Vanzetti went to the electric chair on August 23, 1927.

the minds of the American intelligentsia for years to come and is still far from dead.

THE KU KLUX KLAN

A. Mitchell Palmer's Red Scare of 1919 and 1920 was one manifestation of a growing suspicion that immigrants already in the country were infecting American values, threatening the Constitution, and upsetting the ethnic balance in the population. Opposition to immigrants culminated in the reappearance of an organization that had been disbanded some 40 years earlier, the Ku Klux Klan. From its rural heartlands the KKK used terror to try to preserve a social system that had in fact already changed beyond recognition.

The Reappearance of the Klan

The Ku Klux Klan originally appeared among Confederate Army veterans in the South in the late 1860s, during the postwar Reconstruction period. To preserve white superiority, they terrorized, beat, and killed blacks—and their white Republican supporters—to prevent them from exercising their other new forms of freedom. In 1871 the Force Bill gave federal troops the authority to stop the Klan's activities, and it soon disappeared.

In 1915, however, a former Methodist clergyman named William J. Simmons revived the Klan to uphold white Protestant American values. On Thanksgiving night his supporters gathered on Stone Mountain, Atlanta, Georgia. The Klan tapped into middle Americans' fear that they were being overtaken by the multiethnic population in the towns and cities and their hostility toward "aliens." Membership grew rapidly during the 1920s, from 5,000 to more than two million.

The Klan was politically active and gained influence in numerous states. Its largest membership lay in the North—Ohio had the largest membership of any state—but it was also strong in Midwestern states like Indiana and Illinois.

Violence was never far away, however. There were floggings, kidnappings, mutilations, torture, and murder. Blacks were harassed and intimidated, but most Klan activity in the 1920s was directed against immigrants and Catholics in the North. Most Klan members did not participate directly in violence, but felt that it was justified in order to show their disapproval of gambling or drinking or sexual freedom. They were determined to uphold what they saw as the old moral order. It was a return

to normalcy of a type Harding probably had not considered. In the late 1920s financial and sexual scandals among the Klan's leadership contributed to its rapid decline in popularity.

PROHIBITION AND OLD-FASHIONED VALUES

One manifestation of the general nostalgia for a former version of the United States was Prohibition, which made illegal the manufacture or sale of alcoholic drink. The cause harked back to the religious revivals of the 1820s and 1830s. Various states had outlawed alco-

The Ku Klux Klan parades along Pennsylvania Avenue in Washington, D.C., in this photograph from 1926.

Federal agents in Boston oversee the destruction of wine and spirits in June 1920. Such scenes took place all over the country.

hol in various forms before the Civil War. The Anti-Saloon League was formed in 1893 to campaign against the sale of alcohol. Around 1906 the sale of liquor came under increased attack in numerous states.

The impulse behind the campaign shared similar roots with the return to normalcy: distrust of the cities, where it was thought most drinking went on, and antialien and anti-Catholic sentiments among the rural interests that dominated state legislatures. In World War I a temporary measure halted the making of alcohol to save grain for use as food. In January 1919 the Eighteenth Amendment introduced Prohibition: It became effective a year later.

Prohibition, which supporters called the Noble Experiment, made the manufacture and sale of

A giant beer barrel carries an anti-Prohibition message in 1920: The tax from beer, it suggests, will help balance the national budget.

alcohol illegal for 13 years. It was repealed by Franklin D. Roosevelt in 1933 (see Volume 2, Chapter 2, "The First Hundred Days"). Society split into "wets" and "drys." Drys lived mostly in rural areas

and preached against the evils of alcohol, claiming that Prohibition would instill some sense of morality into the sinful cities.

Wets soon found secret ways of supplying the demand for drink, however. Many people brewed their own beer, ran secret stills, or used industrial alcohol. One man who owned a chain of drugstores in the Midwest bought alcohol legally for medicinal purposes and then hijacked his own trucks.

Bootlegging—the illegal manufacture or import of alcohol—became big business and was the main source of income for criminal gangs in the big cities (see Volume 3, Chapter 5, "Crime in the Depression"). They organized their own supply and distribution networks, corrupted the police and the legal system, and demanded protection money from clubs and

illegal drinking clubs. Law enforcement agencies found it almost impossible to enforce Prohibition. Mabel Walker Willebrandt, assistant attorney general in charge of Prohibition prosecution, admitted that Americans could buy alcohol "at almost any hour of the day or night, either in rural districts, the smaller towns, or the cities."

Prohibition introduced a new kind of organized crime to American cities as gangs emerged to control the supply of liquor. Chicago gangster Al Capone (1899–1947) became rich and powerful on the proceeds of his dealings in liquor, along with prostitution and gambling. Capone traveled in a $30,000 armor-plated Cadillac, protected from rival gangs by his own hoodlums. In the mid-1920s there were 130 reported gang murders in Chicago: The police—

at best ineffectual, and at worst corrupt—did not make a single arrest related to the killings.

4. DANGER SIGNS IN THE ECONOMY

America in the early 1920s was a country of contrasts. Following World War I, the United States had the highest standard of living in the world. Workers were paid higher wages than ever before; labor agitation had brought a reduction in working hours from the standard 12-hour day. In 1926 industrialist Henry Ford, who pioneered the assembly line in his car-making plants, gave his workers a five-day week and paid them $5 per day, twice the going rate. For the first time many workers were entitled to a paid annual vacation.

Mechanization

Mechanization played a large part in the increasing wealth of the nation. Ford announced, "Machinery is the new Messiah." In 1914 he had started production of his automobiles on the first conveyor-belt assembly line, where workers could assemble a car in about one and a half hours. Only a year earlier it had taken around 14 hours.

Electric power replaced steam engines, machines replaced human labor, and productivity soared. New products were developed all the time, including cigarette lighters, reinforced concrete, Pyrex, and rayon. Fruit and vegetables were canned on a large scale. New synthetic materials were devised, partly in response to a shortage of imported natural materials from Europe, such as potash. Substitute

A garter flask displayed by the dancer Mlle. Rhea. The fad was one way of concealing alcohol.

John Barleycorn, symbolizing liquor, has been killed off by the puritans but is resurrected by criminals.

synthetics such as plastics and rayon could be produced relatively quickly and cheaply.

Construction

Cities grew at a rapid rate, and New York City, Chicago, and other centers developed a new skyline composed of skyscrapers. People needed more space in which to live, so construction spread outside city boundaries, creating the new suburbs. This, in turn, allowed real-estate managers to become wealthy. The motor industry, meanwhile, encouraged the construction of a network of new roads and highways.

BIG BUSINESS

During the 1920s more businesses began to merge, sometimes bringing together companies in different cities, while at other times linking rival firms. Between 1919 and 1930 mergers led to the disappearance of 8,000 businesses, of which more than 3,700 were utility companies providing electricity, gas, or water. At the same time, large business concerns emerged, many of which are still household names today, like Chrysler, Colgate, and Maxwell House.

Not everyone benefited from the prosperity of the early 1920s. Wages did not keep pace with shareholder dividends. As many as 42 percent of Americans lived on a wage of less than $1,500 a year, beneath the poverty line. At the same time, most of the country's wealth was concentrated in the top 5 percent of the population.

THE EARNINGS GAP

Despite general increases in the standard of living, the polarization of earnings was increasing. One politician who spoke up for low-paid workers was Fiorello La Guardia (1882–1947), a Congressman from East Harlem (see Volume 4, Chapter 1, "Left vs. Right"). Local people had complained that the price of meat was too high, so La Guardia asked William Jardine, secretary of agriculture, to investigate. Jardine's response was to send La Guardia a leaflet on the economical use of meat. La Guardia fumed: "I asked

Marcus Garvey

Marcus Garvey (1887–1940) led America's first important black nationalist movement. He arrived in the United States from his native Jamaica in 1916 to found branches of his Universal Negro Improvement Association in Harlem and other cities where migration had created new concentrations of black population. By 1919 the "Black Moses" claimed two million supporters for his espousal of black pride and an independent black economy within the U.S. system. He set up a newspaper, *Negro World*, and a black shipping line, the Black Star Line, among other businesses. Garvey alienated labor and socialist leaders, however, by insisting that racial inequality was independent of class inequality; he alienated the established National Association for the Advancement of Colored People by agreeing with the Ku Klux Klan that the black and white races should be kept separate. He was sent to prison for fraud in 1925 and, when released in 1927, deported as an undesirable alien.

An increasingly common sight: a Washington, D.C., office staffed by three young women.

for help and you send me a bulletin. The people of New York City cannot feed their children on department bulletins…. Your bulletins…are of no use to the tenement dwellers of this great city."

The Mellon Plan
A further blow to the poor came in 1923. Andrew Mellon, secretary of the treasury and one of the richest men in America, presented to Congress a program of tax cuts to reduce the rate from 50 percent to 25 percent for top taxpayers and from 4 percent to 3 percent for the poorest. The bill saved Mellon alone $800,000 in tax. Congress passed the plan, however, convinced by the argument that benefits to the rich would trickle down to the rest of society.

Other people recognized the injustices of the system. There were numerous strikes for better pay and conditions. In 1922

Senator Burton Wheeler of Montana investigated the complaints by striking coal miners and railroad men. He was deeply shocked: "All day long I have listened to heart-rending stories of women evicted

●

"The people of New York cannot feed their children on department bulletins."

●

from their homes by the coal companies. I heard pitiful pleas of little children crying for bread. I stood aghast as I heard most amazing stories from men brutally beaten by private policemen. It has been a shocking and nerve-racking experience." Although the early twenties brought a return to normalcy for many, that normalcy was now being challenged.

Harding and Corruption

Harding's presidency ended amid financial scandals and accusations of corruption. The so-called Ohio Gang, from the president's home state, included Harry Daugherty, who had acted as Harding's campaign manager in the 1920 election. As attorney general, Daugherty took bribes for favors, including political appointments and pardons for criminals. Charles R. Forbes, meanwhile, head of the Veterans' Bureau, sold hospital supplies as "surplus" to his friends at as little as 10 percent of what they cost the government. In 1927 Daugherty was tried for defrauding the government but was acquitted.

The biggest single scandal of Harding's term concerned oil deposits beneath Teapot

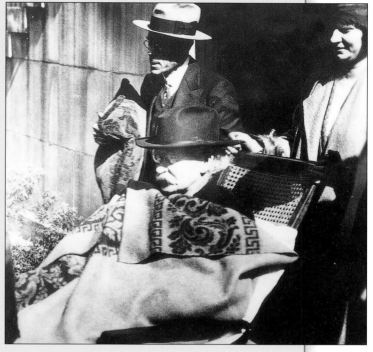

Former secretary of the interior Albert Fall arrives for his trial in 1929. Found guilty of taking bribes, he served a year in prison.

Dome, a rock formation in Wyoming. The reserves had been set aside for the U.S. Navy, but in 1922 they were secretly leased to private business by Harding's secretary of the interior and former mentor, Albert Fall (1861–1944). The two chief beneficiaries, Edward Doheny and Harry Sinclair, were later revealed to have given Fall $105,000 and $304,000 respectively. After years of determined investigation by Senator Thomas Walsh of Montana, Albert Fall was eventually sentenced to prison in 1929, the first time any U.S. politician had been jailed for crimes committed while in cabinet office. Doheny and Sinclair, however, went unpunished.

Harry M. Daugherty, one of the most corrupt politicians to hold government office, escaped conviction for his crimes.

4

THE ROARING TWENTIES

The decade that followed World War I was one of the most eventful and complex periods in the history of the United States. Dubbed the "Roaring Twenties" or the "Jazz Age," it saw America reach the heights of prosperity, then descend into the gloom of the Great Depression.

The 1920s have long been characterized as a decade of frivolity and decadence, an era of nonstop partying and economic prosperity that began with the end of World War I in 1918 and continued until the Great Crash in 1929. The decade is dubbed variously the "Roaring Twenties," "the Age of Excess," "the Jazz Age," or "the Dance Age." Such phrases capture only part of a highly complex era. For many people life was nothing like as entertaining and carefree as the names might imply.

1. TWO SIDES OF THE AGE

The decade was full of contrasts: between rich and poor, between cities and country, between internationalists and isolationists, between conservatives and forward-thinkers. For many Americans the country had never had it so good.

The dynamic economy brought a consumer boom as mass production allowed Americans access to previously unobtainable items. Calvin Coolidge (1872–1933) summed up the philosophy of the age in his famous dictum "The business of America is business." Prosperity encouraged small investors to buy shares in booming

Wing walker Al Wilson plays a golf shot in this photograph from 1924. Such daredevil stunts were typical of the 1920s.

Economic Background

A dynamic economy lay behind many characteristics of the 1920s. The car, radio, telephone, refrigerator, and washing machine became staple possessions in many households. Increases in income levels not only enabled people to buy these consumer items but created more leisure time, which was rapidly filled by the burgeoning radio and magazine industries, by sports, dancing, and later in the decade, by visits to the movie house to see the latest talkies.

F. Scott Fitzgerald, pictured here with his wife Zelda, was the leading chronicler of the Jazz Age. The Fitzgeralds' own glamorous yet tragic life seemed to sum up the complex nature of the era.

firms: From 1923 the stock market entered a so-called bull phase, with constantly rising share prices.

Prosperity was not uniform, however. For farmers, the urban poor, and factory laborers, along with nearly the entire black American population, the 1920s were a decade of hardship and suffering. To buy the new products on the market, many workers worked a 10- to 12-hour day, often with little job security and no health benefits. Although gleaming new Model T Fords might sit outside American homes, they were often bought on extended credit, and the homes themselves often lacked even the most basic plumbing.

Other Americans struggled to understand the consequences of World War I, which had left 10 million people dead, including nearly 100,000 Americans. While politicians led America down a path of international isolation in search of "normalcy" (see Chapter 3, "The Return to Normalcy"),

•

"...grown up to find all gods dead, all wars fought, all faith in man shaken."

•

some Americans were disenchanted with their countrymen. Some criticized America's isolationism and innate conservatism.

Fitzgerald's Decade

The prominent chronicler of the twenties was the novelist F. Scott Fitzgerald (1896–1940), the man who invented the phrase "the Jazz Age." Fitzgerald's works and life, however, portrayed the very complexity of the decade and the loss and confusion behind the façade. Although his five novels and many short stories dealt ostensibly with the glamorous lives of the rich, he saw himself as belonging to a disappointed and confused generation. Of his contemporaries he wrote, "Here was a new generation...dedicated more than the last to the fear of poverty and the worship of success; grown up to find all Gods dead, all wars fought, all faith in man shaken."

Fitzgerald and his wife, Zelda, were prominent members of upper-class society on the East Coast and on the French Riviera. Fitzgerald became famous with books such as *The Great Gatsby* (1925), an evocation of the aimless, decadent lives of the rich. Eventually, however, in an ironic echo of the doomed lives of Fitzgerald's glittering characters, the high living, drinking, and partying took their toll. Zelda went crazy and was admitted to a mental asylum; Fitzgerald suffered from alcoholism and spent the 1930s in Hollywood writing mediocre movie scripts, failing to rekindle the fiery creativity that produced his 1920s novels.

INCREASED URBANIZATION
By 1920 America was, for the first time, an urban nation. More than half the population lived in communities of 5,000 or more. New York was the most populous city, but new centers of industry such as Chicago and Detroit also experienced massive growth.

The change marked the latest stage in America's move away from an agrarian society to an industrial one; it also changed the ethnic balance. A majority of the newcomers were black. In the preceding decade some 500,000 black Americans had left the South and the countryside for the cities of the Northeast. In the 1920s the figure rose to 750,000. In 1890, 1 in 70 people in Manhattan was black; by 1930 it was 1 in 9.

Whites, too, moved to the growing conurbations, but often to the suburbs. There they could own their own house and yard, a dream made possible by mass-produced cars and commuter trains. Housing tended to divide by color. Black families, poorer workers, and immigrants lived in the inner cities. In places such as Manhattan the very rich had their own exclusive housing.

THE ENERGY OF THE CITIES

America's cities were the focus of economic activity, symbolized by new construction work. For much

Builders on a skyscraper pause to look out over New York as evening falls. Construction work characterized American cities in the 1920s.

The Suburbs

As America urbanized, real estate prices in the major cities rocketed, doubling between 1920 and 1926. Suburbs grew rapidly as workers started to look beyond the city limits for more space and affordable housing. After 1922, 40 percent of all construction work was in the suburbs or for other housing. The suburbs and smaller cities across the Midwest, particularly, became home to the white middle classes.

of the decade Manhattan resembled a giant construction site as old buildings were torn down and new ones erected. Improvements in elevator technology and structural steel made it possible to build higher, overcoming the prohibitive price of land by building upward. Corporations built higher to express their own importance. The most celebrated piece of "vanity" building led to the competition between the 1,048-foot Chrysler Building, completed in 1929, and the Empire State Building, which was finished in 1931 and topped 1,250 feet. Across the United States the now-familiar skyscraper skyline started to appear: modern-day Chicago, Kansas City, Los Angeles, San Francisco, Pittsburgh, and Cleveland all took shape during the 1920s.

RURAL AMERICA

Rural America remained important. Some 30 million Americans continued to live on farms, and a further 32 million lived in small towns. During the preceding decade, and particularly during the conflict of 1914 to 1918, farmers had prospered from feeding a nation at war and providing war-torn Europe with grain. Many farmers had gone into debt to buy new machinery to increase production and had been badly hit when the high demand for grain fell once peace was restored. In the 1920s falling demand and good harvests led to a surplus, and farmers found their crops' value slashed. By 1929 wages had fallen below their level in 1920; over the decade more than 1.5 million farmers abandoned their farms for the cities and towns (see Volume 3, Chapter 2, "Shadow over the Countryside").

SMALLTOWN U.S.A.

Political activity was often characterized by a conservatism that seemed at odds with the

H. L. Mencken

Henry Louis Mencken (1889–1956) was a critic and essayist who became known as the "sage of Baltimore." As the author of *The American Language* (1918), a standard work that has since been revised many times, and as editor of the periodicals *The Smart Set* and *American Mercury*, Mencken was one of the most important literary figures in the United States from around 1910 to 1940. He was best known, however, as the most consistent critic of the America in which he lived. Mencken believed that most of rural America was filled with unthinking, undiscriminating people whom he labeled "boobs" and who collectively belonged to what he dubbed the "booboisie."

Henry Mencken was born in Baltimore and began his career as a journalist at the age of 18 on the *Baltimore Morning Herald*. By the age of 25 he had done well enough to take over the position of editor in chief. The paper closed, however, in 1906 and Mencken joined the *Baltimore Sun*, where he worked for the rest of his career, except for leaves of absence during the two world wars.

Mencken quickly became known for his newspaper articles, which he used to satirize and attack American taste and culture. He enjoyed making fun of the many popular beliefs that he saw as ridiculous or absurd. His caustic wit singled him out as a writer to be feared as much as enjoyed. At the same time, however, he published more academic works on playwright George Bernard Shaw and German philosopher Friedrich Nietzsche.

In 1908 Mencken began to write book reviews for the magazine *The Smart Set*. By the end of his career at the periodical he had written more than 2,000 reviews. From 1914 to 1923 he was joint editor of the magazine, which he helped establish as the arbiter of literary taste throughout the United States.

In 1923 Mencken became founding editor of the *American Mercury*, a collection of humorous observations of customs and politics aimed at sophisticated readers. The periodical brought Mencken to the height of his influence. In 1925 he attended the Monkey Trial in Tennessee (see box, page 59), where he criticized the fundamentalist lawyer and politician William Jennings Bryan as the epitome of the small-mindedness that he believed bedeviled the United States. Mencken had to flee Dayton to avoid being run out of town by the very inhabitants he lampooned for being small minded. When Bryan died at the end of the trial, he penned a vicious obituary for which he refused ever to apologize.

A portrait of H. L. Mencken by Carl Van Vechten. Known for his investigations into American linguistics, Mencken coined phrases such as "It is a sin to believe evil of others, but it is seldom a mistake."

carefree image of the Jazz Age. "Red" scares, race riots, the Ku Klux Klan, anti-immigration laws, and a decline in the power of unions were all signs of a preference for values that harked back to an older or imagined United States.

The novelist Sinclair Lewis (1855–1951) satirized small-town America and its conservative attitudes in his best-selling novel, *Babbitt* (1922). The book is set in the fictional Midwestern city of "Zenith," home to 250,000 inhabitants whose dedication to the getting of money Lewis sees as an embodiment of American philistinism (see box, page 61). Zenith's white, middle-class inhabitants show a total disregard for politics and worship business-

Author Sinclair Lewis, pictured in 1925, was a relentless critic of what he saw as small-minded small-town attitudes.

men and the economy, thus mirroring the attitudes of most employed lower- and middle-class Americans during the 1920s.

For Lewis and other critics of American attitudes another sign of conservatism came in the Scopes Monkey Trial of 1925, when a teacher was accused of teaching Darwin's theory of evolution (see box, opposite). Journalist H. L. Mencken, the decade's most outspoken critic of America (see box, page 57), called the assembled fundamentalists at the trial "gaping primates" and an "anthropoid rabble." Mencken's criticism of Bible-Belt America was so harsh that it looked as though he would be run out of town: He left of his own volition.

When the fundamentalist lawyer W. J. Bryan dropped dead five days after the end of the trial, Mencken wrote a vitriolic obituary, "In Memoriam: W.J.B.," in which he attacked Main Street

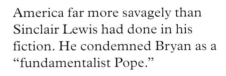

Business over Politics

For many middle-class Americans the successful businessman was a hero to be respected and, if possible, emulated. It had always been part of the American psyche to admire those who built their own business. During the 1920s the admiration of the American worker for business was increased partly by the lackluster nature of politics. Both presidents Harding and Coolidge made it clear that they rated business as more important than politics. F. Scott Fitzgerald observed: "It was characteristic of the Jazz Age that it had no interest in politics at all."

America far more savagely than Sinclair Lewis had done in his fiction. He condemned Bryan as a "fundamentalist Pope."

The Ku Klux Klan
The rise of the Ku Klux Klan in the early part of the decade, in Mencken's eyes, only proved rural America's lack of wisdom or virtue. Calling for 100 percent Americanism, the KKK restricted its membership to native-born white Protestants and rallied against Catholics, Jews, immigrants, black Americans, and Native Americans, all of whom it accused of not being true Americans. The organization's membership soared from 5,000 to around four million in 1924 as it grew from its southern base to states

"The Monkey Trial"

One of the most memorable expressions of the clash between modern and conservative America came in May 1925 in Dayton, Tennessee. High-school science teacher John Thomas Scopes was tried for illegally teaching Charles Darwin's theory of evolution, which proposed that humans had evolved from earlier apelike life forms. The Scopes Monkey Trial, as it became known, was the first trial broadcast on radio and attracted every major journalist in the country. It was a sensation.

Scopes, the defendant, was a bit player in the trial. The key men were his defense lawyer, Clarence Darrow (1857–1938), an avowed agnostic and the most controversial lawyer of the time, who fought to uphold the concept of freedom no matter how un-popular his clients, and the counsel for the prosecution, William Jennings Bryan (1860–1925). Bryan was a three-time presidential candidate and former secretary of state who had turned his back on politics and become the leader of a fundamentalist movement. The trial was a duel between two erstwhile friends, pitching the agnostic against the religious fundamentalist. In the court of law Bryan won: Scopes had broken Tennessee's proscription against the teaching of evolution and was duly found guilty. He was fined $100. In the wider context, however, Darrow proved the victor. He exposed Bryan's creationist beliefs as ill-founded and illogical. Nevertheless, the law remained on the statute until the late 20th century.

such as Illinois, Indiana, Pennsylvania, and Ohio, the last with the highest Klan membership that year. The revival of the traditional-ly rural KKK was another indication of the gulf between the cities and the country (see Volume 5, Chapter 2, "Equality for Some").

CREDIT AND ADVERTISING

By 1925 many firms were overproducing consumer goods for a market that was already full. The people who might have provided new markets for such goods—farmers, blacks, Native Americans, unskilled and seasonal workers—were excluded by low wages. For those without ready cash a new type of payment was introduced, initially by car dealerships: credit on installment. Consumers could buy major purchases and pay back the cost, plus interest, in a series of installments at set intervals. In 1929 $3 billion worth of goods were bought on credit.

The pressure on consumers to buy, even if it meant going into

Cars line a small-town main street in Ohio. For observers such as Mencken, such communities embodied the petty-minded, intolerant, sometimes racist attitudes of rural America.

A poster advertising Mobiloil. The car culture spawned new industries such as oil and gas.

debt, grew as producers became better at promoting their goods. The advertising industry expanded rapidly on the back of the growth in consumer items. In order to persuade Mr. Andy Consumer—a name used in a campaign promoting the benefits of advertising—to keep buying, advertising stressed the benefits of technological advances. Print advertising appeared in every paper and magazine; advertising and product sponsorship of shows soon spread to radio.

THE GOLDEN AGE OF MOTORING

By 1929 there was a car for every five Americans, and most families owned one. Such high levels of ownership brought in their wake extensive road-building programs, gas-station construction, and the emergence of a whole roadside scenery of advertising billboards and motels.

The amount of paved road in America doubled during the 1920s, the so-called "golden age of motoring." Building and maintaining highways cost more than $1 billion a year. Highway building became the biggest single cost for the nation and employed more workers than any other sector of the economy. The car's constant need for gasoline also helped transform the developing oil business into a huge industry.

WOMEN AND NEW WAYS OF THINKING

Following the Great War American society witnessed a radical change in manners and morals. Soldiers and nurses, returning from Europe, found themselves questioning accepted values, partly because they had been exposed to the horrors of war, and partly because their experience of continental life caused them to rethink their own lives. Innovative thinkers, such as the Austrian pyschoanalyst Sigmund Freud (1856–1939), added to the climate of change by introducing new perspectives on human nature itself.

Nowhere was change more visible than in the position of women. During the 1920s the appearance and attitudes of women were transformed. The words "feminism" and "feminist" were coined in New York City to express the new attitudes. Generations of women had dressed in ankle-

The Auto Companies

At the start of the 1920s, although there were 44 different auto companies in the United States, Ford dominated the market. In 1909 Henry Ford had introduced the Model T to early success, particularly because it was sturdy enough to drive over the unpaved roads that existed before the highway-building program. In 1924 Ford produced 1.5 million closed Model T cars at their lowest-ever price of $290. By fall the next year Ford was producing one car every ten seconds.

Ford replaced the Model T with the Model A in 1927 in the face of competition from rivals such as Chrysler and General Motors. General Motors offered a range of cars, from the cheap Chevrolet to the more exclusive Cadillac, each in a range of colors. The firm's head, Alfred P. Sloan, realized that increasingly sophisticated car buyers wanted choice. Unlike Ford, Sloan offered the consumer not only choice but the concept of obsolescence: Every model was superseded by a newer version each year. By 1930 six companies had emerged to share 90 percent of the automobile industry, employing directly or indirectly some three to four million workers.

The Traveling Salesman

Sinclair Lewis's 1922 novel *Babbitt* satirized the "hustler" mentality of American businessmen, mocking the worship of success and the unending, immoral quest for money. George Follansbee Babbitt, the book's hero, was a "shambling, seriocomic figure" with a "cash-and-carry measurement of success."

Of the numerous "Babbitts" in the America of the 1920s, many were traveling salesmen. Around the mid-19th century the traveling salesman, or commercial traveler, was almost unknown. The relative scarcity of most manufactured goods created a ready demand for their producers. Increased production and improvements in transportation created more goods that required more aggressive selling methods: The traveling salesman took to the roads. Around 1869 there were probably only 1,000 or so traveling salesmen. By 1900 the number had risen to 92,919.

As business competition grew fiercer, sales methods became more aggressive. "High-pressure" selling techniques were used to move products for which there was no great perceived need. That meant training salesmen to do more than present a product. Traveling salesmen soon became notorious for their glib tongues and the stories with which they softened up their targets, steering them toward purchases they did not need. So low fell the salesman's reputation for immoral dealing that training was introduced to improve their ethics.

length skirts, tight corsets, and high-necked blouses. By the 1920s the long skirt, corset, and layers of clothes had gone, replaced by shorter skirts, dropped waists, and short hair. Shoulders, arms, and knees became visible.

The new sense of freedom mirrored an increasing independence and assertiveness. During the war women had worked in large numbers, and many continued once the war ended. In the twenties women usually worked in white-collar jobs, as clerks, cashiers, and switchboard operators.

In cities like New York women cropped their hair into the "bob" cut, which was often hidden beneath a cloche hat. With their short hair and short skirts, turned-down hose, and makeup, this young and self-confident group of women became known as "flappers," a name that possibly related to the sound of their skirts flapping as they danced. The typical flapper liked to party and,

no longer bound by tradition, to smoke, drink, kiss in public, and just as shockingly, apply makeup in public. Previously makeup had been largely considered immoral. As a result the cosmetics industry boomed, and beauty parlors opened up all over the country.

The flapper helped define the era. Zelda Fitzgerald, wife of author F. Scott Fitzgerald, said of the flapper, "She flirted because it was fun to flirt and wore a one-piece bathing suit because she had a good figure, she covered her face with paint and powder because she didn't need it and refused to be bored chiefly because she wasn't boring. She was conscious that the things she did were the things she had always wanted to do."

The silent film star Louise Brooks (1906–1985) epitomized the flapper. Her popularity—she even inspired the comic strip *Dixie Dugan*—was a reflection of the age's preoccupation with youth. Her social life centered

around many of the era's key artistic and literary people, including Anita Loos (1893–1981), who wrote two novels about a flapper, *Gentlemen Prefer Blondes* (1925) and *Gentlemen Marry Brunettes* (1928).

2. POPULAR CULTURE

Black culture enjoyed a renaissance, based on Harlem. Between 1920 and 1930 the number of blacks living in Harlem doubled from 100,000 to 200,000. The dynamism of the area attracted writers such as the Missouri-born poet Langston Hughes (1902–1967). Hughes' poetry was inspired by local people, including an elevator man and a prostitute, showing how they bore their lives with dignity and humor. James Weldon Johnson (1871– 1938), who edited the pioneering *Book of American Negro Poetry* (1922), called Harlem "the Mecca for the sightseer, the pleasure seeker, the curious, the adventurous, the...

ambitious, and the talented of the entire negro world."

Black culture flowered despite growing racism and the exclusion many blacks felt from the technological and economic progress of the decade.

THE DANCING CRAZE

Like much cultural and artistic creativity of the period, the dance called the Charleston was purely American. It originated in black culture and debuted in New York in the 1923 revue *Running Wild*. The dance quickly caught on: It was possible to buy Charleston dresses, which swung as the wearer moved. Other dances, such as the Black Bottom, the Lindy Hop, and jazz dancing, also became crazes.

A cartoon depicting the new freedom for women. A flapper applies makeup in public.

Marathon dances, a form of endurance test, became popular. The first marathon was held in March 1923 and won by Alma Cummings, who danced for 27 hours. Within a year the record was 87 hours, although the effort killed the man who set it, Homer Morehouse. Marathon dancing continued into the thirties, when it became a way of earning some money in the Depression. Many people criticized the spectacle as exploiting the desperation of the poor for the prize money for the entertainment of the better off.

THE JAZZ SCENE

F. Scott Fitzgerald took the name "Jazz Age" from the musical form that became synonymous with the time. Jazz originated in New Orleans, where African Americans improvised a music that derived its influences from Europe and Africa. After the large-scale black migration north Chicago became the new headquarters of the music. The craze spread to New York's Harlem by the mid-1920s, when clubs such as the famous Cotton Club presented jazz every night. Harlem became known as the "nightclub capital of the world," with around 125 clubs playing black jazz to a mainly white audience. By the late twenties black musicians appeared on major radio networks and record labels. White Americans well beyond America's urban centers

bought phonograph recordings by leading jazz musicians such as the trumpeter Louis "Satchmo" Armstrong (1901–1971) and the bandleader Duke Ellington (1899–1974).

The term jazz captured the energy of the age. It was increasingly applied to other creative forms that had little in common

The Flapper

The noted Manhattan wit Dorothy Parker wrote a poem called "The Flapper."

The playful flapper here we see,
The fairest of the fair.
She's not what Grandma used
* to be –*
You might say, au contraire.
Her girlish ways may make a
* stir,*
Her manners cause a scene,
But there is no more harm in
* her*
Than in a submarine.

She nightly knocks for many a
* goal*
The usual dancing men.
Her speed is great, but her
* control*
Is something else again.
All spotlights focus on her
* pranks.*
All tongues her prowess
* herald.*
For which she well may render
* thanks*
To God and Scott Fitzgerald.

Her golden rule is plain
* enough—*
Just get them young and treat
* them rough.*

A couple dance for an audience of bemused young black boys. Although many white Americans were eager to seize on elements of black culture, such as the Charleston, racism remained common in U.S. society.

beyond the fact that they belonged to the time and shared a certain modern approach. The seminal poem "The Wasteland" (1922), by the self-exiled poet T. S. Eliot (1888–1965), was reckoned part of the jazz movement because of its innovative construction, for example. The popular tunes produced by the songwriters of Tin Pan Alley were also often included. The composer George Gershwin (1898–1937) wrote *Rhapsody in Blue* in 1924 and fused elements of jazz with both classical and popular music (see Volume 5, Chapter 4, "The Arts in the Depression").

FADS AND CRAZES
Many other fads of the twenties sprang up and disappeared almost as soon as they had arrived. One of the more bizarre crazes was for flagpole sitting. It started when a friend of Alvin "Shipwreck" Kelly

Harlem's famous Cotton Club was one of the most important venues for the pioneers of jazz in the 1920s.

(1893–1962) dared him to climb a flagpole and sit on top of it. He did and stayed there for 13 hours and 13 minutes. Kelly's antics captured the public's attention, and the craze took off. Kelly's record was broken many times over, often by himself. He held the record of 49 days when the

craze disappeared in 1929. During his seven weeks on top of the pole he did not eat any solid food, only drinks hoisted up to him on a pulley. A crowd of up to 20,000 gathered to watch.

Other crazes spread across America. Wingwalking, like flagpole sitting, was an attempt at novelty. Stunts such as two people playing tennis on the wings of an airplane temporarily captured national attention, but the American public was becoming more sophisticated, and the craze failed to take hold.

Games and pastimes were a different matter. In 1923 the East Asian board game Mah Jong was all the rage. Women dressed in Chinese costumes and held Mah Jong parties, wealthy people bought sets costing $500, and a

"Shipwreck" Kelly waves from a flagpole in 1930.

Mah Jong league of America was formed. The crossword craze proved the longest lasting. In 1925 two publishers, Richard Simon and Max Schuster, had the idea of collecting crossword puzzles in book form. Although crosswords had been around for 10 years, this was the first time they had been collected. The book became an instant best-seller and a national obsession. Millions of Americans spent every free moment doing puzzles. In Chicago a woman took her husband to court for ruining their marriage by spending all his time on crosswords. The judge limited the man to no more than three puzzles a day.

RADIO COMES OF AGE

The technological advancements that characterized the decade in business shaped America's new leisure industries. The twenties saw radios become common in homes and the movie industry transform itself with the evolution of the "talkies." Commercial radio broadcasting started in 1920, when Westinghouse's station KDKA in East Pittsburgh came on air. There had previously been little interest in the medium apart from some amateur radiomakers; but once KDKA started to broadcast, radio fever took hold. By 1927 there were some 681 stations. In 1929 between four and five million radio sets were sold; by then more than 10 million families owned a radio. The Radio Corporation of America (RCA)— a joint venture by Westinghouse and General Electric in 1919— dominated the field after it began to mass produce sets in 1921.

National Networks

The National Broadcasting Company (NBC) started the first national radio network in 1924. Now Americans at home across the country could listen to sports events, news broadcasts, the Scopes Monkey Trial, or President Coolidge speaking from the White House. Such shared experiences had the incidental effect of making the country seem smaller and more closely knit. Advertisers, realizing the huge potential audience, were quick to use the new medium to sell their products.

One of the most popular radio shows ever started in 1928. The *Amos 'n' Andy Show* was about two blacks from the south side of Chicago. Played by white actors, Amos was a happy-go-lucky, simple guy, while Andy was lazy and bossy. Although the comedy was based on crude racial stereotypes, it was the most popular show in the nation, listing the president among its listeners. There were few more telling illustrations of the gulf between white and black Americans. It became a TV show in the 1950s.

THE MOVIES

Advancements in the movie industry during the twenties possibly had an even bigger impact on American social life than the radio. Throughout the decade Americans flocked to movie theaters, which became ever grander, more lavish picture palaces. At the start of the decade silent movies dominated the screen, featuring stars such as Charlie Chaplin (1889–1977) and Rudolph Valentino (1895–1926). Silent movies, accompanied by a live piano, became slicker, with elaborate costumes and stage sets, as the early movie tycoons started

•

"Valentino had silently acted out the fantasies of women all over the world."

•

to realize the industry's potential. By 1926 the movies were the fifth-largest business in America. Audiences, visiting theaters several times a week to see the latest releases, wanted to be entertained and to escape into a fantasy world. Actors and actresses became stars, enjoying glamorous lifestyles principally in Hollywood, California, the main home of the industry. Movie studios also exis-

Two sides of a new phenomenon: the radio. A whole group of friends gathers in a living room to share the experience of a broadcast (above), while a stylish young woman demonstrates the radio as fashion accessory, posing with her portable set on the beach (below).

ted in New York City. As late as 1929, 24 percent of movie production was still based in the city.

When Rudolph Valentino, the star of *The Sheik*, one of Hollywood's biggest successes, died unexpectedly in 1926 at the age of 31, the country was gripped by an unprecedented wave of public grief. The line of mourners who visited the funeral home to pay their respects stretched for 11 blocks. The actress Bette Davis summed up Valentino's appeal, "Valentino had silently acted out the fantasies of women all over the world. Valentino and his world were a dream. A whole generation of females wanted to ride off into a sandy paradise with him."

The Talkies

The technology for producing movies with sound existed as early as 1921, but studio bosses were unsure how audiences would react to the innovation and so continued to produce silent movies until 1927. The first "talkie" premiered on October 6, 1927, when Al Jolson (1886–1950), a singer-comedian, who in the fashion of the day performed with his face "blacked," starred in *The Jazz Singer*. It was an immediate hit and changed movies forever. Not all of the silent movie stars survived the transition to the talkies. Actors such as the romantic star John Gilbert saw their careers end because their voices proved unsuitable for the new medium.

The cinema boomed, however. Audiences rose sharply from 60 million to 110 million. By the end of the decade the musical had become the dominant form, and three out of every four Americans went to the movies each week. They wanted to see a new movie every time. The industry grew rapidly, and with it the Hollywood star became established (see Volume 5, Chapter 5, "Hollywood: The Depression Years").

Many actors who had started out on the New York theater stage traveled to Hollywood to make their fortune. They included the Marx brothers, Cary Grant, Fred

Astaire, Ginger Rogers, Clark Gable, Humphrey Bogart, Bette Davis, Katharine Hepburn, and Mae West.

THE THEATER

Despite the drain of acting talent to Hollywood, live theater thrived, particularly on the East Coast. New York's theater scene exploded in the twenties as city audiences flocked to performances. By 1926 New York had almost 70 theaters, most of which were located around Broadway between 28th and 50th streets. The average number of plays staged at any one time in the decade was 225, a rate that has never been equaled.

THE MEDIA

Along with theater and jazz New York City was also home to another cultural phenomenon of the decade, the proliferation of quint-essentially urban and urbane magazines. In the first decade of the media age magazines, book clubs, and best-seller book and record charts proliferated alongside the talkies, radios, and phonographs. Magazines such as *The New Yorker*, *Vanity Fair*, *American Mercury*, and *The Smart Set* were read all across the country. Publishing and printing became the second largest industry in New York City in the 1920s after textiles.

American Mercury was launched in 1924 by H. L. Mencken and George Nathan to explore what Mencken called "the whole gaudy, gorgeous American scene." The magazine was more likely to be read by college students and those who liked to think of themselves as free thinkers. It actively encouraged new talent and promoted rebelliousness, and was highly regarded by writers such as F. Scott Fitzgerald. *The New Yorker*, launched in 1925, became the

most influential magazine of its generation and remains one of the country's major magazines today. It attracted the decade's best writers, such as the humorist James Thurber (1894–1961), and became famous for its witty and original cartoons. The magazine embodied the same spirit that jazz music also captured: It was smart, slick, and urban. The writers wrote as Americans and used their own personalized English.

At the Algonquin Hotel in Manhattan, close to *The New Yorker* offices, the magazine's staff used to meet regularly. Around what became known as the "round table" gathered wits like Dorothy Parker

A magazine cover from 1926 illustrates a couple doing the Charleston, a dance popular with the new publications' urbane, urban readership.

(1893–1967), Robert Benchley (1889–1945), and Alexander Woollcott (1887–1943). They helped create a new American voice that was echoed in other publications such as *Reader's Digest* and *Time*, both of which continue to be read all across America.

Not all magazines were aimed at the fashionable urban classes. With increased leisure time, many Americans could read more magazines. Young women looked to titles such as *Good Housekeeping* and *Ladies Home Journal* for hints and advice that their mothers would once have dispensed. Advertising in such publications defined the aspirational middle-class lifestyle for which most white

Babe Ruth became the first real "sports personality" in America and a household name.

Americans worked and which installment payments seemed to place within easy grasp.

The twenties was also the golden age of pulp magazines catering to all genres. *Tarzan* first appeared in the 1910s and 1920s. In 1923 *Weird Tales* became the world's first fantasy magazine; it was followed in 1926 by *Amazing Stories*. The first science-fiction

magazine, *Amazing Stories*, demonstrated the genre's popularity by quickly reaching a circulation of 100,000 to 150,000 per issue.

The Tabloids

Tabloid journalism also boomed during the 1920s. People developed an insatiable appetite for gossip and sensationalism. Murder trials, and love and sex stories gripped the nation. In 1927 the trial of a housewife from the New York borough of Queens, Ruth Snyder, and her lover for the murder of her husband received more column inches in U.S. newspapers than the controversial execution of the anarchists Sacco and Vanzetti, which occasioned worldwide interest and condemnation (see box, page 47).

3. SPORTS

Many Americans became fascinated by the behavior of anybody in the public eye. The New York Yankees' most famous player, Babe Ruth, deserves much of the credit for transforming baseball into a popular spectator sport and also for creating celebrity sports personalities. At the time baseball was a low-scoring game, with most runs made from single hits; the game had also suffered from score-fixing scandals. Ruth's hitting transformed the game into a thrilling spectacle.

George Herman "Babe" Ruth (1895–1948) began his career as an outstanding pitcher. When he went to play for the Yankees in 1920, they wanted him in the outfield, where he would play every day, rather than pitching, where he would appear only every three to four days.

In his first Yankees season, 1920, he doubled the home-run record of 27, set in 1884, with 54. In the 1921 season he hit 59 home

Jack Dempsey poses in a fighting stance at a training camp in a photograph from 1922.

runs and scored a total of 177 runs. His 1927 record 60 home runs were not beaten until 1961. Such was the excitement of watching the Babe play that attendance doubled, and the Yankees had to build a new stadium in 1923. Yankee Stadium is still known as "the house that Ruth built."

Radio made the Babe one of America's most famous personalities, and the media reported his glamorous lifestyle. He could do no wrong for a public appreciative of his charity work and visits to orphanages and hospitals.

Jack Dempsey

Another sportsman who became a hero thanks to radio was the boxer Jack Dempsey (1895–1983). Boxing was widely considered

sleazy until 1919, when Dempsey fought Jess Willard for the heavyweight championship. The fight transformed the sport; henceforward fights were held in respectable venues and people like John D. Rockefeller sat at ringside. In 1921 Dempsey fought the first prizefight to gross over $1 million.

The most famous fight of the twenties was Dempsey's 1927 rematch with Gene Tunney, who had taken his title the previous year. Americans were glued to their radios as Dempsey knocked Tunney down in the seventh round. Tunney got to his feet on the count of eight and went on to win. Dempsey supporters accused the referee of staging a "long count" so that Tunney could recover.

GAMES AND PASTIMES

Tennis and golf, previously the preserve of the wealthy, became popular as Americans enjoyed participating in sports and games. Tennis courts and golf courses were built throughout the country. College football expanded rapidly as a spectator sport.

At home Americans found new pastimes. General knowledge quiz books, such as *Ask Me Another*, became all the rage. Self-help books also became popular. The most famous was by Frenchman Emile Coué (1857–1926). In 1923 his *Self-Mastery through Conscious Auto-Suggestion* hit the best-seller list. Coué advocated a system of popular psychotherapy based on the repetition of a daily mantra: "Every day in every way, I am becoming better and better."

THE CREATIVE LIFE

American artists and writers sought consciously to break with the past. This meant creating work that was wholly American and did not look to Europe for ideas or

approval. In art forms such as architecture Americans had imprinted their own ideas on the international scene. The architecture of Frank Lloyd Wright (1867–1959) and the skyline of skyscrapers were wholly American. In painting Georgia O'Keeffe (1887–1986) was beginning to create a style that would set the stage for many artists to follow.

Literature showed continued uncertainty about the future (see Volume 5, Chapter 6, "Chroniclers of the Great Depression"). Many writers disliked the money-oriented attitude of such works as the 1925 best-seller *The Man Nobody Knows: A Discovery of the Real Jesus*. Author Bruce Barton cast Christ as the embodiment of 1920s business values.

The Lost Generation saw America as a moral wilderness, where gangsters ran businesses, minor personalities were worshiped, and racism flourished. Writers including T. S. Eliot, Ezra Pound (1885–1972), and Ernest Hemingway (1899–1961)—whose 1926 novel *The Sun Also Rises* was about disillusioned expatriates living in Europe—fled across the Atlantic, particularly to Paris.

SEE ALSO

◆ Volume 1, Chapter 3, The Return to Normalcy

◆ Volume 1, Chapter 5, The Fantasy World

◆ Volume 5, Chapter 3, Society in the 1930s

◆ Volume 5, Chapter 4, The Arts in the Depression

◆ Volume 5, Chapter 5, Hollywood: The Depression Years

Charles Lindbergh

During the 1920s, the American public embraced a range of heroes who, through the constant coverage of the various media, in some ways became as familiar as members of their own family. Among them was Charles Lindbergh (1902–1974). Several pilots had successfully crossed the narrow northern region of the Atlantic Ocean, but nobody, to date, had flown from New York to Paris. A $25,000 prize was offered for the first successful solo crossing. Six pilots had died in 1926 and 1927 attempting to win the prize when a 25-year-old former stunt pilot, Charles Lindbergh, turned up in New York announcing his intention of flying solo to Paris in a small plane. By the time his specially built monoplane *Spirit of St. Louis* finally took off on May 20, 1927, Lindbergh had grabbed the nation's imagination. The previous failed attempts had been made in much larger airplanes with much better-known pilots; Lindbergh's attempt seemed to be madness.

Lindbergh, however, was both disciplined and well-trained. Having calculated the exact load the airplane could carry, he ditched all unnecessary weight—including his parachute and radio—and took with him only five sandwiches and a thermos flask for the journey.

With careful navigation—although at one stage when he saw a fishing boat, he flew down and yelled to the crew, "Which way is Ireland?"—and sheer willpower Lindbergh flew the plane to Paris in 33½ hours. He landed on a Parisian runway and was completely unprepared for the reception he received; more than 100,000 people turned up to cheer the man the press called "Lucky Lindy." His reception back home in New York City was even more remarkable. He was showered with 1,800 tons of tickertape as he paraded through the city in an open-topped car.

Charles Lindbergh became an all-American hero, praised not only for his feat but also for his wholesome character as a good-looking, clean-cut, nonsmoking teetotal-

ler, an unlikely hero for the Roaring Twenties and another reminder of the conservatism that underlay its more brilliant surface. In later life Lindbergh suffered tragedy when his baby child was kidnapped and murdered in 1932. The case caused a sensation in the United States. Bruno Hauptmann, a German-born carpenter, was arrested and executed for the crime in 1936 (see Volume 3, Chapter 5, "Crime in the Depression").

The publicity surrounding the kidnapping drove the Lindberghs to flee to Europe. There Lindbergh was criticized for his links with the Nazi Party in Germany, which the Nazis exploited against his will for publicity purposes. In World War II, however, he actively supported the United States. As a civilian consultant for the United Aircraft Corporation, he flew 50 combat missions against the Japanese in the Pacific.

5

THE FANTASY WORLD

Toward the end of the 1920s it seemed nothing could halt America's prosperity. Confidence in the business sector was never higher, and there was money to spend. Caution was thrown to the wind, however, and too much was produced, while the rush to get rich on stocks led to disaster.

In August 1923, when United States president Warren G. Harding died, Republican vice president Calvin Coolidge (1872–1933) was sworn in to take his place, the sixth vice president to become president on the death of the chief executive. The following year Coolidge was elected in his own right to a four-year term.

Famous for his reluctance to waste words, "Silent Cal" Coolidge may seem out of place in the heady, verbose "Jazz Age." In many ways, however, the new president harked back to established

Calvin Coolidge takes the oath of office in his father's home in Plymouth Notch, Vermont, where he was on vacation when President Harding died. He was sworn in in front of witnesses by his father, a notary, to become the 30th president of the United States.

American traditions of rural common sense and pithy wisdom. He had set out his approach in a speech to the Massachusetts Senate in 1915, when he advised his listeners to "Be brief; above all things, be brief." He only issued public statements when he felt they were absolutely necessary.

1. "COOLIDGE PROSPERITY"

Calvin Coolidge's term in office from 1923 to 1929 coincided so closely with the height of apparent economic prosperity that the era came to be known as "Coolidge prosperity." The foundations of prosperity were apparent to many

The Election of 1924

In 1924 the Democrats and the Progressive Party formed to advocate a reformist program in the election both urged a vote against the Republicans in light of the scandals of Harding's presidency (see Chapter 3, "The Return to Normalcy"). The Republicans retaliated with the slogan "Keep cool with Coolidge." Coolidge and his running mate, Charles Dawes, went on to receive well over half the popular vote. Coolidge won 382 electoral votes, compared to 136 for Democratic candidate John W. Davis. In the popular vote he registered 15,717,553, compared to 8,386,169 for Davis. The new president's inauguration speech was the first broadcast by radio.

observers. Two major surveys caught Americans' sense of living during a significant period. In their 1925 study of an Indiana town Robert and Helen Merrell Lynd concluded, "We today are probably living in one of the eras of greatest rapidity of change in the history of human institutions." The Lynds had also, however, documented great poverty and class divisions in the town.

In 1933, when a committee on social trends reported its findings after four years' work, it expressed admiration for advancements that "have hurried us dizzily away from the days of the frontier into a whirl of modernisms which almost passes belief."

Among other advancements of the 1920s the report listed the electrical industry, the growth in car ownership, and the emergence

•

"...a whirl of modernisms which almost passes belief..."

•

of the radio and movie industries. There were other developments: in technology—refrigeration and food canning, mechanization; in social organization—Prohibition, woman suffrage, and birth control; and in the economy—mass

Macy's department store on 34th Street, New York, became an icon of the consumer world.

production, advertising, and credit systems (see Chapter 4, "The Roaring Twenties").

The economy was booming. Within a few years of the end of World War I in western Europe in 1918 the United States was producing more goods than the world's other six leading economic nations combined. Manufacturing productivity increased by 32 percent between 1923 and 1929. Between 1925 and 1929 the number of manufacturing companies grew from 183,900 to 206,700, while the value of the goods they produced rose from $60.8 billion to $68.0 billion.

For many Americans the good times showed every sign of getting better and better. Literature and education increased in importance: As the number of children in employment fell to only 1 in 20 by 1930, school attendance increased. Air travel became available to more people.

COOLIDGE'S CHARACTER

Coolidge had grown up in Maine, where he absorbed lessons of self-dependence and frugality. After college he became a lawyer and a city councilor, the basis for a career in politics driven by the desire he explained to his father: "I want to be of use in the world, and not just get a few dollars together." Testy and taciturn, he nevertheless had a spirit of fun. In the White House he played jokes on the staff and three times a day rode on an electric artificial horse. Warned that he might become a laughing stock, he replied, "It's good for people to laugh."

Coolidge made his national political reputation in 1919, when as governor of Massachusetts he called out the National Guard to help break a strike in the Boston police force. Soon after, he famously declared in a telegram to labor leader Samuel Gompers (1850–1924), "There is no right to strike against the public safety by anybody, anywhere, any time."

A LAISSEZ-FAIRE TRADITION

In the Republican tradition of *laissez-faire*, or the free market, Coolidge believed that the key to prosperity lay in minimal government interference in the life and business of the country (see Chapter 1, "The United States, 1865–1914," and Volume 4, Chapter 1, "Left vs. Right"). His government spent most of its budget on interest payments on the nation's war debts and on benefits to veterans of the conflict, and little on anything else. His view of the government's role was clear when he claimed, "If the federal government should go out of existence, the common run of people would not detect the difference in the affairs of their daily life for a considerable length of time."

In keeping with such beliefs, Coolidge made it clear from his first address to Congress in December 1923 that his government would barely become involved in the economy beyond offering its general support for business. In the pithy sayings for which he was renowned he later famously observed, "The chief business of the American people is business," and "The man who builds a factory builds a temple; the man who works there worships there." In keeping with such attitudes he preserved protective tariffs for industry and opposed investigations into the tax affairs of big corporations. The man he appointed to run the Federal Trade Commission in 1925, intended to regulate American business, himself condemned the commission as "an instrument of oppression and disturbance and

Coolidge and Nicaragua

In international affairs Calvin Coolidge maintained the practice of "dollar diplomacy" in Latin America. Like his predecessors, he used U.S. forces to protect U.S. business interests. U.S. troops had landed in Caribbean or Central American states 20 times from 1898 to 1920. In 1912 they landed in Nicaragua, partly to prevent a rumored Japanese plan to build a canal across the Central American isthmus, which would have challenged the Americans' Panama Canal.

President Harding withdrew the troops in 1925, and a coup quickly followed. Coolidge feared that Mexico was trying to spread communism in the region. He sent in 2,000 troops to restore to power Adolfo Díaz, a conservative former president. At the same time he sent lawyer Henry Stimson (1867–

1950), later secretary of state under Herbert Hoover, to get support from Mexican-backed rebels led by José Maria Moncada. Stimson met the rebel general and argued the U.S. case. He wrote, "In less than thirty minutes we understood each other and had settled the matter." Moncada laid down his arms; part of his reward came two years later, when he became president himself.

One of Moncada's fellow liberal leaders, Augusto Sandino, declared "We will never live in cowardly peace under a government installed by a foreign power." He led guerrilla raids against the U.S. Marines until they left in 1933. He was killed the following year but remains a hero to many Nicaraguans; members of the leftist National Liberation Front are sometimes known as Sandinistas.

injury." Coolidge also reduced taxes and introduced legislation to further restrict child labor.

Coolidge was determined to limit federal spending and balance the budget. He refused to support the development of hydroelectric generating stations on the Tennessee River or Herbert Hoover's plans for river control projects in the West—both policies adopted in the early 1930s— because they were too expensive. The same was true of providing relief for the nation's farmers and speeding up the payment of bonuses promised to veterans of World War I. When the European Allies tried to make new arrangements for paying back the $10 billion they had borrowed from the U.S. government, he refused, saying, "They hired the money, didn't they?"

Andrew Mellon, secretary of the treasury under Coolidge as he had been under Harding, prom-

Misguided Optimism

Coolidge's State of the Union address of December 1928 often draws accusations of complacency, given the approaching crisis. He said: "No Congress has met with a more pleasing prospect than that which appears at the present time. In the domestic field there is tranquillity and contentment...and the highest record of years of prosperity." He predicted that the country should "anticipate the future with optimism." Coolidge, like other observers of the time, believed in the importance of political and business leaders encouraging confidence.

Children play in a New York pool in the late 1920s. Such pools were a sign of greater public prosperity.

oted fiscal policies to benefit business. The rich paid one-third less tax in 1926 than they had in 1921. Mellon believed in encouraging large corporations with tax breaks and reducing the tax burden on the wealthy. Their increased spending would "trickle down" to the lower levels of the economy and stimulate reinvestment.

2. ECONOMIC WEAKNESS

For all its apparent success Coolidge prosperity was built on fragile foundations. Mass production, one modern scholar notes, depends on mass consumption; in other words, there must be customers for goods. But the huge increase in manufacturing productivity in the 1920s was not matched by rises in wages, which

A Sears Roebuck advertisement urges Americans to "own your own home." Advertising boomed in the 1920s as businesses had to compete strongly for consumers.

went up by an average of only 8 percent in the decade. Mechanization cost millions of jobs: At the height of Coolidge prosperity unemployment in manufacturing industries ran at 10 percent. Although industries such as construction and auto-making boomed, traditional 19th-century industries, such as railroads, textiles, shipbuilding, leather, lumber, flour-milling, and coal mining, suffered from underemployment and unused capacity. Many workers in such industries found their living conditions worsen; they were often laid off for long periods. Those who did work commonly put in up to 48 hours a week, including Satur-

days. The two-day weekend off work was not yet common. With no vacation pay or pensions, vacations and retirement were too expensive for many workers.

Coal and Cotton

The introduction of manmade fibers such as rayon meant that cotton mills found it hard to be competitive, particularly since the price of raw cotton fluctuated wildly. Mill-owners found the easiest way to cut costs was to cut labor costs. In the Southern heartlands of the U.S. cotton industry in the 1920s, women, children, and impoverished tenant farmers were used as a source of cheap labor. The workers were mostly nonunionized, illiterate, and poor. Layoffs were a normal feature of working life in cotton mills and coal mines, where productivity rose 8 percent while wages fell 14 percent, resulting in strikes and violence.

Across the decade as a whole, average wages barely rose. In 1920 the average wage was $1,424; in 1929 it had only risen to $1,489, but the cost of living had risen quicker. The near-stagnant wages prevented the creation of wealth that would increase the market for goods. The market for cars, refrigerators, and other consumer goods became saturated.

URBAN VS. RURAL

Other signs of economic weakness lay in the discrepancy between America's urban and rural popu-

lations. While city-dwellers enjoyed many technical advances, the 50 million Americans who still lived in the country were excluded from prosperity. Few had electricity; around 45 million of them did not have indoor plumbing. A woman from the Texas hill country remembered making trips to the outhouse in the dark: "I had a horrible choice of either sitting in the dark and not knowing what was crawling on me or bringing a lantern and attracting moths, mosquitoes, nighthawks, and bats."

Farmers struggled as prices tumbled and surpluses grew. They

Hoover's Worries

Future president Herbert Hoover served as Coolidge's secretary of commerce and found himself often at odds with his boss. Although he later gained a reputation for nonintervention during the Depression, Hoover was an early advocate of federal intervention for farm relief or works programs. Coolidge vetoed them on the grounds of cost. Hoover said that the president's attitude was that nine out of ten troubles would "run into the ditch" before they arrived. Hoover went on, "The trouble with this philosophy was that when the tenth trouble reached him he was wholly unprepared." For his part, Coolidge was just as damning of Hoover: "That man has offered me unsolicited advice for six years, all of it bad."

and their families could take little part in Coolidge prosperity. Coolidge twice vetoed, moreover, a bill passed by Congress that would make the government the "buyer of last resort." The McNary-Haugen Bill would have committed the government to buying up agricultural surpluses and selling them off abroad, injecting money into the rural economy.

In the cities, meanwhile, new magazines like *Time* and *American Mercury*, the latter published by social commentator H. L. Mencken (see box, page 57), reflected a new sophistication and cultural superiority. To many city-dwellers rural America was the home of ignorant fundamentalists. Author Sinclair Lewis mocked the rural world in *Elmer Gantry*, published in 1927.

TROUBLE IN THE CAR INDUSTRY

Even the car industry, a success story of the early decade, displayed signs of weakness. They were made worse because it supported many other industries. Car manufacturers bought about 80 percent of America's rubber production, for example.

During a minor depression in the early 1920s car sales dried up, and General Motors' stock tumbled. Founder and chief executive William Durant—who in 1919 had introduced installment buying to persuade customers to make purchases—left the company in 1923 and was replaced by Alfred P. Sloan. Sloan developed a number of techniques to encourage trade. By far the most significant was his drive to stimulate sales by changing model styles every year, or what some observers later called planned obsolescence. The idea was to convince customers to buy a new car before the old one had

worn out or, effectively, before they needed to. Sloan used advertising to reinforce his message: GM spent more than $20 million on advertising during the decade. He also set up a group management system that was better equipped to deal with very large companies.

Nevertheless, in 1926 General Motors conceded that a saturated market would bring an end to rapid expansion of car sales. A

New England Vacationland. In the urban centers of the East Coast prosperity allowed the middle classes to live comparatively luxuriously, with modern conveniences at home and vacations.

report predicted, "…the volume has now reached such large proportions that it seems altogether unlikely that tremendous annual increases will continue."

People Would Buy Anything!

At the height of the Florida real estate boom of the mid-1920s the frenzy of speculation was such that incautious investors bought anything they thought might make a profit. This led to a number of situations in which sales were sometimes fraudulent, and buyers did not get quite what they bargained for.

One of the most common ruses was to lie about the exact location of a development. Bostonian Charles Ponzi, for example, developed a subdivision that was supposedly near Jacksonville in the north of the state. In fact it was 65 miles away from the thriving city, but Ponzi did a roaring trade.

Manhattan Estates, meanwhile, offered lots that lay only three-quarters of a mile from the fast-growing city of Nettie. What better prospect could there be for the investor, whose land values could only increase as the city expanded? The only weakness in the plan was that the city of Nettie did not exist.

Meanwhile, the congestion of road and rail traffic into the state became so acute that eventually only essential freight was let in. What was most often designated as essential freight? It was the building materials for developing more subdivisions.

The New York Stock Exchange in the 1920s. Playing the market was the preferred form of speculation for many Americans.

The next year Henry Ford closed his plant for some months, ostensibly to change over production from the Model T to the Model A. The closure led to a fall in the Federal Reserve Index of Industrial Production but had no effect on the market. The *New York Times* Industrials, an index of the share values of top industrial companies, reached a high of 245 by the end of the year.

Ford's Model A went on to outsell GM's Chevrolet, and the two companies remained the leading car makers, with Chrysler third. Many other smaller manufacturers went to the wall. The need to offer credit to sell cars increased the motor companies' debts, however. After the Wall

Street Crash in October 1929 production of all vehicles fell by 36 percent in 1930 (see Chapter 6, "The Crash of 1929").

The credit installment system itself weakened the economy. When customers bought on extended credit—some $3 billion of goods were bought on credit in 1929 alone—businesses ran the risk of bad debt or, in some ways just as bad, of having to repossess unpaid-for goods for which they had no prospective repeat buyers. By the middle of 1929 U.S. businesses had stockpiled some $2 billion worth of goods in their storerooms, waiting for buyers.

THE FLORIDA LAND BOOM

One of the most graphic examples of the overheating economy came in the land rush in Florida. The boom began in the 1910s when Florida's growing reputation as the Sunshine State attracted increasing numbers of Northerners. Land grew increasingly valuable, particularly from Miami north to Palm Beach and across to the west coast. Land developers were quick to take advantage as investors flocked to the state. Stories abounded of people who traded their last few dollars for real estate that was soon worth a fortune. Salesmen were quick to latch on to potential investors, transporting them around the state, buying them meals and

drinks to persuade them into buying a plot of land.

By the mid-1920s names like Miami, Miami Beach, and Coral Gables had come to symbolize rapid profits for many Americans. The attraction of the state's climate to Northerners was undeniable—economist John Kenneth Galbraith said that their annual trip to the sun was "as regular and impressive as the migration of the Canada Goose"— and that seemed to guarantee real estate as a no-lose investment.

The people who bought property at the start of the boom

Exciting Times

A journalist met a woman in Florida whose account captures the heady excitement of the times: "Came with a special party two weeks ago. Bought on the third day. Invested everything. They guarantee I'll double by February. Madly absorbing place! My husband died three weeks ago. I nursed him over a year with cancer. Yet I've actually forgotten I ever had a husband. And I loved him, too, at that!"

Miami's drydock had only been finished shortly before the Florida hurricane of September 1926: This is how it looked afterward.

were the ones who benefited. As more people became involved, speculators were increasingly involved in a race to buy up land before the flood of newcomers to the state dried up. This played into the hands of the real estate agents. Investors sometimes bought without even having seen the land, only some architects' plans. Some of the land they bought proved to be swamp or otherwise unsuitable for development.

Land could be bought for a downpayment of only 10 percent of its value, with a relatively lengthy delay before signing the legal contract made the next in a series of payments necessary. Prices rose so rapidly that some people were able to sell at a profit before the first payment even became due. Such was the demand that some plots changed hands up to 10 times within a couple of years. The purchasers had little intention to live on their land, simply to make a profit.

Through 1925 speculators continued to flood the state, which became increasingly subdivided by developers. The term "beach property" came to be used to describe anything that lay between 10 and 15 miles from the sea.

The Oklahoma City business district, photographed in 1930. Business districts and the high-rise buildings that characterized them were physical signs of urban prosperity.

The End of the Boom

In 1926 the supply of buyers for land in Florida began to diminish, mainly as a consequence of the overheated market and of the inability of the state's railroads to cope with the influx of visitors. Then, in September a hurricane hit the state, killing 427 people and leaving many thousands injured or homeless. Another storm struck later in the fall.

Some people believed that the storms had brought a healthy break in the boom, which would pick up and carry on as before. They were wrong: The boom was at an end. Bank clearings in Miami in 1925 totaled $1,066,528,000; in 1928 they had dropped to $143,364,000. A large percentage of property was not paid for and returned by default to its original owners. By now, however, much had been transformed from farmland, fruit groves, or swamp to residential developments. For Floridians the land rush had had environmental as well as economic consequences. For other Americans, meanwhile, the ominous symbolism of the storms in Florida failed to dent their optimism that the U.S. economy would keep growing and support them all. If land investment failed, there was always the stock market.

3. THE STOCK BOOM

The stock-market boom began in 1924, when the price of shares began to rise perceptibly; they went on rising into 1925. Investors rushed to buy shares in companies that would either yield them a dividend—a portion of a company's profits—or that they would be able to sell at a profit if the firm did well. The *New York Times* average of prices, given in a point system, rose steadily, with only a few minor drops during the period. The average price of 25 industrial stocks in May 1924 was 106. By December 3, 1925, it stood at 181. The value had risen by more than two-thirds.

The next year, 1926, saw a slight drop in the market. Some people believed this was a correction that simply reflected the fact that values had risen too quickly the year before. March 1926 saw the *Times* Industrial Average fall to 172 then slip again to 143 at the end of the month. Another minor blip occurred in October—it coincided with the hurricanes in Florida—but failed to stop the general rise in share prices. By 1927 Herbert Hoover, secretary of commerce, was condemning what he later called "an orgy of mad speculation."

Supporting Europe

Economic developments overseas had an undermining effect on the U.S. economy. The countries of Europe were struggling to rebuild their economies after the war and to pay the vast debts they had run up during the conflict. In 1925 the then British chancellor of the exchequer, Winston Churchill, returned his country to the gold standard. The standard was an economic device used to regularize international finance by linking the value of a country's that gold moved easily from Britain to the United States as debt repayment. At the same time, Britain negotiated new loan agreements with American banks that also increased the flow of funds into the United States.

The result in America was to make more money available in the economy. Interest rates, meanwhile, were high. This was good for investors, who received a good return on their money and so kept their investments in America rather than in Europe or Britain. Adding to the international problem was the United States' insistence on high tariffs, taxes imposed on imported goods in order to protect domestic industry. The Fordney-McCumber Tariff Act of 1922, for example, which restored tariffs to their prewar levels, discouraged European exporters and prevented American consumers' benefiting from cheap imported goods and lower prices.

Interest Rates

To many people in Europe and America it was important for the United States to help halt the flow of gold from Britain to America in order to stabilize the world economy, which was still recovering from the effects of World War I. The easiest way to do this, they argued, would be for the United States to drop its interest rates. This would discourage saving and encourage overseas investment.

One of the most important supporters of such a policy was Benjamin Strong, governor of the New York Federal Reserve Bank. The Fed is the United States' central bank system, established to control and regulate the country's money supply; the New York branch is the most powerful bank in the system.

Candy-maker Wrigley's joined the advertising boom: The package and logo remain similar today.

currency to the amount of gold it possessed. Churchill returned Britain to the gold standard at its prewar level. That meant that the pound sterling was now worth $4.86, compared to a rate of $3.66 in 1920. The move vastly overvalued the pound. It hampered British exports by making them cost more, but encouraged overseas suppliers to import goods into Britain. The gold standard committed Britain to exporting gold if there was no other way to pay for those imports or for its other foreign debts. The result was

John Maynard Keynes

The attempts by the Federal Reserve to manage the economy were praised by British economist John Maynard Keynes (1883–1946). Many people regard Keynes as the most important economist of the 20th century.

Born into a prosperous and academic family, Keynes studied at Eton and Cambridge. He worked at the British Treasury during World War I and came to public attention when he wrote *The Economic Consequences of the Peace* (1919). The book criticized the Versailles Peace Settlement for crippling the German economy and thus European recovery after the war.

In 1925 Keynes criticized Britain's return to the gold standard; persistent unemployment throughout the 1920s also forced him into conflict with orthodox free-market economics when he began to promote public works schemes to get the unemployed off welfare.

When the Depression struck in the 1930s, conventional economists still believed that the workings of the free market would eventually solve the problem. Keynes argued against this in an important book, *The General Theory of Employment, Interest and Money* (1936). He proposed that in a depression wages would never fall so low that they would eliminate unemployment. The problem was caused not by high wages and prices but by low demand. Keynes saw demand as originating not just from private consumers but also from investors and public agencies, such as governments. Business investors and public agencies had the real power to stimulate demand and thus increase employment. Rather than waiting for a depression to end, Keynes argued, governments could spend their way out by investing in public works projects and giving subsidies to consumers. Policies of lower interest rates and easy credit would also serve to stimulate business investment.

Keynes' theories, called Keynesianism, were adopted by many countries during and after World War II. They committed themselves to maintaining high employment in order to preserve prosperity. Many economists still accept Keynes' emphasis on macroeconomics, or the study of an economy as a whole, though his theories have been modified.

John Maynard Keynes was a fellow of Kings College, Cambridge, and worked at the British Treasury during World War I.

Strong was influenced by economist J. M. Keynes (see box). He was enthusiastic about Keynes' idea that governments should manage the money supply, which some observers saw as too much government intervention.

Supply and Demand

For classical economists the boom of 1927 and 1928 contradicted the principle of supply and demand. It held that prices rose and fell according to how many goods were available and how many people wanted to buy them, thus regulating the economy. By cutting interest rates, such economists argue, the Fed put more money into the economy, kept prices artificially high, and thus depressed demand.

EUROPE'S BANKERS

In 1927 Montague Norman, governor of the Bank of England, Hjalmar Schacht, the governor of the German Reichsbank, and Charles Rist, deputy governor of the Bank of France, traveled to America to discuss the possible lowering of interest rates. They met with Strong in spring at the Long Island estate of Treasury undersecretary Ogden Mills.

Both the German and French bankers were concerned that lowering U.S. interest rates would be inflationary. Norman and Strong disagreed, and Strong pressed the Fed into dropping its rediscount rate—the rate at which it loaned money to banks—from 4.0 percent to 3.5 percent, thus injecting money into the economy. The Fed also bought government securities, again putting cash into circulation. The policy had many critics. Herbert Hoover dismissed Strong as "a mental annex to Europe." Adolph C. Miller, a member of the Federal Reserve Board who disagreed with the

The demand for cars increased, but in many cases roads remained little more than tracks.

move, said it was "the greatest and boldest operation ever undertaken by the Federal Reserve System and...resulted in the most costly errors committed by it or any other banking system in the last 75

•

"...the most costly errors committed by it or any other banking system..."

•

years." In hindsight Miller would be proved right.

From 1921 to 1929 the U.S. money supply remained largely stable. The price index, an index of consumer prices, showed a rise from 93.4 in June 1921 to 104.5 in

Cars parked on the roof of a Buick sales and service building. Business was booming.

it to eager investors at a rate of 10 percent or more. Business corporations were equally quick to see the potential profits in lending money to stock investors. Standard Oil, for example, loaned millions of dollars every day.

DOWNSIDE

Critics of the Federal Reserve maintain that it should have tightened the availability of credit in 1927 and 1928 as stock-market speculation reached its height. Such criticism largely ignores the

November 1925 and then a drop back to 95.2 in 1929, showing that prices had remained about the same over those years.

It seemed as if the Federal Reserve Board's deliberate control of economic growth through price stability had been a success. Keynes described the Fed's management of the dollar as a "triumph." However, the Fed's actions also made borrowing easier by making more money available. Credit expanded by 68 percent between 1921 and 1929. The Fed encouraged borrowing by keeping rates low and making cheap, uneconomic loans to foreign countries.

Where Did the Money Go?

Part of the problem was that little of the cash the Fed injected into the economy actually went to consumers to increase their purchases of manufactured goods, as economic theorists would have

wished. Instead, some of it went on capital investment in machines, labor, and premises. Manufacturers produced more goods, many of which went straight into warehouses where they remained, unbought.

Much of the money that banks loaned went to buy stocks. The rise in the value of stocks in 1927 and 1928 promised rich returns. The call-loan method of buying—in which investors bought shares for a small downpayment and took out a loan for the rest of the cost, which they hoped to pay back by selling the shares before the loan fell due—appeared to make playing the stock market relatively low risk (see box, page 92).

In 1928 some 38 percent of loans made by banks went toward buying securities to play the market. Those banks could borrow money from the Federal Reserve at a low rate of 3.5 percent, then lend

A Warning Voice

James Adams, a respected historian and former Wall Street businessman, wrote an analysis of American business in the mid-1920s that maintained that prosperity was an illusion and a state of mind. He predicted a crash unless drastic reforms tackled the weaknesses of the economy. Adams pointed out that numerous industries were suffering and that among the supposedly prosperous ones only a few were healthy. He criticized the notion of ever-expanding growth. Expansion cannot go on unhindered based on the assumption that high wages will increase consumer power, which in turn creates increased production. If wages fell, expansion would cease. The crash proved Adams right.

complexities of the situation, however. Money had been cheap before, and yet there had been no wave of speculation to resemble that of 1928 and 1929: Cheap money alone did not make the crash inevitable. Other factors included upheavals in the international finance system after the end of World War I, and particularly following Britain's decision to return to the gold standard.

Economists are still unable to pinpoint a precise reason for the Great Crash. One important factor was simply the atmosphere of the times. As in the Florida real estate boom, people were anxious to speculate and were convinced that investment offered a way to easy wealth. It seemed that anyone was entitled to their share of the Coolidge prosperity. In 1928 the market began to rise in leaps and bounds only to drop then leap even higher. A key period in the onward rush was March 1928, when the industrial average rose 25 points in a month. Radio and other stocks made spectacular leaps. To those willing to see it, the world of economics and expectations had less and less to do with the real world, of goods, sales, and money.

VOICES IN THE WILDERNESS

While investors were being urged to put more and more money into the market, some people saw the storm clouds brewing. Early in 1929 one New York bank warned of bad consequences "if the rate of credit increase rises above the rate of business growth." Others, like James Adams (see box, page 82) worried about how real America's prosperity actually was.

INFLUENCE

Among the other factors that stoked stock-market activity were the actions of the large corporations themselves. Some businesses fraudulently inflated their own worth to attract investors. Others worked in a more subtle way by maintaining the general air of confidence. John J. Raskob (1879–1950), director of General Motors and later chairman of the Democratic National Committee, was known as a shrewd operator

Vacuum cleaners on display in a store. New homeowners had to have this time-saving device.

A Popular President

While on a fishing vacation in South Dakota in 1927, Calvin Coolidge summoned reporters to a school he used for press conferences. In virtual silence he handed each of them a small strip of paper. All the strips bore the identical message, "I do not choose to run for president in nineteen twenty-eight." The announcement came as a great shock—even the president's wife did not know it was coming. Everyone believed that Coolidge would have been reelected easily. Some observers suggested that he might want to be urged to run again. When Herbert Hoover was elected, Coolidge began to refer to him somewhat bitterly as "the wonder boy."

Coolidge was highly popular in the United States for bringing honesty and probity back to the White House after the shady dealings of the Har-ding administration became known. He was also noted for his dry wit and famous reluctance to use more words than necessary. It was said that an actress sitting beside him at dinner once turned to him and said, "Mr. President, I've just made a bet that I can get you to say more than two words." Coolidge replied, "You lose." When it came time to leave the White House in 1929, Coolidge supervised the packing himself. Surveying the boxes of effects, he joked, "I am having rather more trouble in getting out of the White House than I had getting in."

Coolidge's reputation suffered as the Depression bit. He got some blame thanks to his policies of easy credit, high tariffs, and lack of support for farmers. Society wit Dorothy Parker was particularly cruel, however, when she was told in 1933 that Coolidge had died and asked, "How can they tell?"

in the stock market. In March 1928 he told the press he had high hopes for the automobile industry in general and General Motors in particular. GM shares were then trading at 187. Raskob's optimism caused a flurry of buying; on March 24 GM shares gained five points, the following week they went up to 199. The surge prompted a further surge in the market generally.

Other major players also helped maintain the value of the market. They included William Crapo Durant, former GM officer turned stock-market speculator, Canadian-born speculator Arthur W. Cutter, the Fisher brothers of the Fisher Body Company, and the Dupont family, famous now for the chemicals they manufacture.

Other factors that encouraged speculation were the huge increase in margin trading and the emergence of a whole group of new investment trusts. Margin trading allowed buyers to acquire stocks without paying for them. Brokers loaned money to buy stocks they then kept as collateral on the loan. The purchaser profited from dividends or a rise in the value of the stocks while avoiding paying the full price for them.

Dividends were low, however, because they are a share of the real profits earned by a business; few businesses were returning significant profits in the late 1920s. Average dividends were about 1 or 2 percent of the investment, compared with an average of 4.5 across the last century. Speculators were dependent on the value of shares rising so that they could sell, pay back the original loan, and pocket a profit. Buying on margin vastly encouraged speculation.

Brokers' loans amounted to over $6 billion at the end of 1928. The return on them had been a healthy 5 percent at the beginning of the year; by its end it had reached 12 percent. This was very good indeed and resulted in a rush of money into Wall Street. The banks had a vested interest in keeping speculation going. They could effectively borrow from the Federal Reserve Bank at 3.5 percent interest, then relend the money at 12 percent.

By the end of 1928 investment trusts were appearing at the rate of one a day. They placed investments on behalf of a whole number of customers, giving even modest investors a chance to become involved in the markets. The trusts soon produced huge paper growth. The United Founders Corporation, for instance, began with $500 and in a short time was valued at $686,165,000. Such growth was based on only very small real returns, however. The trusts only added to the scale of speculation,

To listen to election results, President Coolidge had a radio installed in his railroad car.

making the whole system even more frenzied.

It has been argued that the banks should have intervened on margin trading and the trusts by upping interest rates. But they were also trapped. By 1929 they were speculating themselves, often in their own stock.

OVERPRODUCTION

The New York stock market crashed in October 1929. Many observers have been tempted to see the crash as the instigator of the Great Depression that followed. Today most economic historians see the crash as only partly to blame. The real causes had been present in the economy for some time. The main problem was overproduction and lack of consumption. There were fewer buyers for consumer products: Those who had money had bought what they needed; those without could not afford to enjoy the consumer goods that stacked up in showrooms and warehouses.

Disparity in wealth was shown to be not just a social problem but an economic one. Poverty led to borrowing, repossession, and bankruptcy. Once the lower-paid consumer stopped purchasing, the results were reflected upward. Middle-income storekeepers and factory owners lost buyers and in turn lost income, causing them to cut down on purchasing. The result was recession and then the Great Depression.

6

THE CRASH OF 1929

Wall Street witnessed one of the world's great stock-market disasters when the New York Stock Exchange crashed in 1929. The crash was the result of weakness in the American economy, and although not the root cause of the Great Depression, it was intimately linked with its beginning.

The latter part of 1929 was one of the most turbulent periods in U.S. financial history. One of the most calamitous slumps of all time, the New York stock-market crash of October 1929 directly or indirectly affected millions of people. In the words of economist John Kenneth Galbraith (1908–), October 30 was "the most devastating day in the history of the New York stock market and it may have been the most devastating day in the history of markets." The repercussions of the crash would contribute to the disruption of the world economy in the 1930s. In the United States the three years after the crash were a downward spiral of misery and destitution as millions were thrown out of work. As increased import tariffs restricted international trade, the crisis grew into the worst depression the world had known (see Chapter 7, "Hoover: The Search for a Solution").

The crash followed a period of unparalleled prosperity during the 1920s (see Chapter 5, "The Fantasy World"). Many U.S. citizens had enjoyed a standard of living that they could hardly have imagined at the start of the decade.

The key to this boom was a tremendous increase in productivity resulting from new technologies. During the 1920s, for example, in response to the rapid depletion of resources following World War I (1914–1918), the chemical industry developed a range of artificial textiles and plastics, such as rayon and cellulose. All of them became important industries. More remarkable still was the rise of the electrical industry and the development of

•

> *"It may have been the most devastating day in the history of markets."*

•

new sources of power. The 1920s also saw the advent of radio, aviation, and countless other technological innovations, all of which would change the fabric of U.S. society forever.

One of the major contributions to the business boom was the automobile revolution. The famous Model T Ford, developed by Henry Ford (1863–1947), brought automobiles to the masses. In 1920 around nine million cars were

registered in the United States. By 1929 the figure was just under 27 million, around one car for every five citizens. The industry's contribution to the national economy was far greater than these figures suggest. Textiles, steel, oil, and construction all prospered as a result; and to many workers in these industries this prosperity brought substantial gains in the form of wage increases, profit-sharing, pension plans, and improved working conditions. These employees found themselves in the unusual position of having money to spend and the time in which to spend it. In more traditional industries, meanwhile, workers saw their purchasing power eroded.

1. BOOM AND BUST

Numerous observers had already begun to warn that the prosperity had no solid footing before, almost overnight, the world's richest and most powerful nation was plunged into financial ruin. Economists now generally accept that the great boom of the early and mid-1920s was built on shaky foundations. Put simply, the capacity to produce had overtaken the capacity to consume. Many parts of the workforce, such as farmers and workers in the

By the time this photograph was taken, in 1924, New York's Wall Street was established as the financial heart of the United States.

declining industries, were outside the general prosperity of the era. Just 5 percent of the U.S. population received a third of the nation's total income by 1929; 71 percent received incomes of less than $2,500 per year, the minimum considered necessary for a comfortable existence. Even some people who were better off than they had been before were unable to afford consumer goods to support mass production.

BANKING AND TIME PURCHASE

The U.S. banking system was also faulty. Unlike most other industrialized countries, the United States still had large numbers of independent banks, many of which were small banks with limited assets. Incompetent regulation, clumsy and dishonest management, and the fact that only a third of banks were members of the Federal Reserve Board—the central banking system set up to regulate and underwrite banks—meant that many were extremely vulnerable. No fewer than 5,000 had failed during the 1920s.

A Personal Account

Alec Wilder, a banker's son who became a musician, was living at New York's Algonquin Hotel. He recalled how he began to suspect that something was wrong with the stock market and a meeting he had with the family's financial adviser:

"I knew something was terribly wrong because I heard bellboys, everybody, talking about the stock market. At the Algonquin they were grabbing as much as they could—horse betting, anything—and running to put this money on margin. It sounded nutty to me....

"I talked to this charming man and told him I wanted to unload this stock. Just because I had this feeling of disaster. He got very sentimental: 'Oh, your father wouldn't have liked you to do that.' He was so persuasive, I said OK. I could have sold it for $160,000. Six weeks later, the Crash. Four years later I sold it for $4,000....

"I wasn't mad at him, strangely enough. But I wanted nothing to do with money. The blow had fallen, and it was over. I was very skeptical and never invested. I became tired of people telling me: 'Oh, there's this marvelous thing happening, and if you should have any extra money....' I'd say, 'Don't talk to me about the market.' I would have nothing to do with it."

Fragile Banks

One of the contributory factors to the weakness of the American economy in 1929 was the banking system. Many U.S. banks reflected the scattered towns in many parts of the nation, operating on a purely local scale. Some had assets of as little as $25,000. Others had loaned to investors to speculate on the stock market and now found it impossible to recoup their losses. Bank failure was inevitable.

A further element of instability came from the rapid expansion of time purchase, or buying on installment, which sustained buying power for a time but could not last forever. At the same time, the Federal Reserve Board's low-interest, cheap-money policy encouraged lending, not least for stock-market speculation. Stockbrokers were lending their own clients money to buy stocks. Meanwhile, unsold goods were piling up in warehouses due to lack of consumer demand. The combination of these weaknesses paved the way for an economic failure.

DELUSION OF HEALTH
The delusion of financial health was prolonged for some by the vigor of the stock market. Secretary for Commerce Herbert Hoover, however, labeled that vigor an "orgy of mad speculation."

Scaffolding covers the new headquarters of the New York Stock Exchange in a sketch of its construction in 1921.

The boom began in earnest in 1927, when the *New York Times* Industrial Average—an indicator that averaged out the prices of a basket of leading stocks—reached 245 points. This marked a net gain of 69 points, or around 25 percent, from the start of the year. Speculative mania seized large numbers of people who had never played the stock market. A "get-rich-quick" atmosphere fueled the relentless purchase of stocks, often "on margin." The margin system allowed investors to purchase stocks without paying for them in the hope that they would yield profits before payment became due. This flood of speculation boosted stock prices hugely. In March 1928 the industrial average rose a further 25 points.

Such rises bore no relationship to the increasing value of industrial

Where Were the Bankers?

The "Big Six," the consortium of six of New York's leading bankers, convened two meetings on Black Tuesday: one at midday and one later in the evening, following the closure of the New York Stock Exchange. Their failure to step in during the day and save the market from total collapse made the banks prime targets for blame. What made the banks' position worse was the suggestion that instead of acting to steady the market, they had actually been liquidating stock themselves, thus adding to the downward spiral of the crash. Chair of the consortium, Thomas W.

Lamont, denied the allegations: "The group has continued and will continue in a cooperative way to support the market and has not been a seller of stocks."

This must certainly have contradicted the gut reaction of at least one member of the consortium. Albert H. Wiggin of Chase National Bank was thought to have lost several million dollars over the course of the day's trading. In any case, the ineffectiveness of the consortium at preventing the disastrous events of Black Tuesday had more or less brought an end to their respected role in economic affairs.

Job applicants wait to be interviewed in the New York Stock Exchange in early October. Right up to the crash, prospects for the exchange looked healthy.

firms or the size of the dividends they would pay on their stocks. Many businessmen remained optimistic, however. In March 1928 the influential John J. Raskob (1879–1950), director of General Motors, gave an optimistic prediction of the prospects for automobile sales for the year and in particular for GM's share of the business. Raskob's optimism about such an important industry sent the whole market into a frenzy of activity. Not only did General Motors shares gain heavily, they set off a flurry of trading elsewhere in the market.

Lending Rise

In January 1929 the *New York Times* Industrial Average gained some 30 points. Stockbrokers' loans to clients had risen to over $260 million, meaning that much of the

trade in stocks was funded by credit. The alarming rise in lending prompted the Federal Reserve Board to issue a press release calling for "Members...to restrain the use, either directly or indirectly, of Federal Reserve facilities in aid of the growth of speculative credit."

Further meetings held by the Federal Reserve Board in Washington, D.C., made the stock market fearful that the Fed was about to

abandon its policy of cheap credit. On March 26, 1929, a remarkable 8.2 million shares were sold on the New York Stock Exchange as people tried to turn their speculations into cash. Thousands of investors saw the value of their investment drop to an all-time low.

March 29, 1929, could itself have been the start of the Great Crash, but for Charles E. Mitchell (see box, page 99). Mitchell was a successful investment banker and,

The quotation room of the New York Stock Exchange, shown in 1928: Traders use telephones to convey news of prices.

more importantly, director of the National City Bank. Mitchell issued a statement to the press suggesting that the Federal Reserve would maintain the policy of cheap credit. Indeed, the banks were speculating on the stock market themselves and did not wish to lose their investments. They would lend money to keep the value of the market high. The stock market had little reason to fear a change of policy by the Federal Reserve Board.

By the fall of 1929 the prices in the stock market were becoming so out of touch with reality that some of the larger, more experienced, speculators began to liquidate their holdings. In mid-September prices fell sharply but then swiftly

recovered. Then, on Wednesday October 23, everyone wanted to sell. The stock market opened fairly quietly, but soon the volume of trade was phenomenal. In the last hour of trading alone 2.6 million shares exchanged hands. Confusion spread as the telegraphic ticker that flashed transactions to traders across the country fell nearly two hours behind actual changes in prices. The *New York Times* Industrial Average dropped from 415 to 384, losing in hours months of accumulated gain. More than six million shares changed hands over the course of the day, prices plummeted, and over $4 million disappeared off the value of the market.

2. BLACK THURSDAY

The next day, now commonly dubbed "Black Thursday," saw an avalanche of sell orders at the New York Stock Exchange as investors

rushed to get rid of their shares. Following a fairly quiet opening, the market rapidly plunged downward in wave after wave of panic-stricken selling. Over the course of the day's trading a record 12.9 million shares were exchanged. The low prices at which most shares were sold shattered the optimism of all those who had owned them.

Initially, prices were firm, but soon a massive volume of shares was being exchanged, and as a result, their prices soon began to fall to record lows. The sheer volume of traffic left the telegraph ticker in perpetual catch-up, and in the uncertainty that followed, share prices fell further and further. By 11:00 A.M. the market had collapsed into a frenzy of selling. News of the collapse traveled faster than the lagging ticker, and uncertainty led to more and more selling. Boardrooms

The Ticker Machine

When stock prices began to fluctuate rapidly, it became a problem for brokers outside the exchange to receive up-to-date information on which to base their decisions. They relied on tickers, machines that recorded on thin paper tape details of all transactions and prices. The ticker had been introduced in 1867, replacing human messengers. In the Great Crash tickers failed to keep up with the volume of deals, making information permanently out of date and intensifying the mood of panic.

were left speechless as share values fell far below those of previous slumps. By 11:30 A.M. the financial community was in uproar. Black Thursday was all but over by noon.

PANIC AND MYTH

Crowds gathered outside the New York Stock Exchange on Broad Street. Police arrived en masse on Wall Street to ensure the peace. All over the United States similar crowds formed around the branch offices of the larger brokerage firms. Speculation in the market was matched by speculation as to what was happening inside the New York Stock Exchange. Rumors were rife. The Chicago and Buffalo stock exchanges had closed, some people said; share prices had plunged to nothing. A persistent myth began with many stories of ruined men and women

killing themselves: Already 11 well-known speculators were said to have thrown themselves out of their high-rise windows.

THE BANKERS ACT

Something had to be done, and something was done. At noon news reporters learned of a meeting at the headquarters of bankers J. P. Morgan and Company at 23 Wall Street. The meeting was attended by some of the most powerful bankers in the country, including Charles E. Mitchell, chairman of the board of the National City Bank; Albert H. Wiggin, chairman of the Chase National Bank; William C. Potter, president of the Guaranty Trust Company; Seward Prosser, chairman of the Bankers Trust Company; and the consortium's chairman, Thomas W. Lamont, senior partner of J. P. Morgan and Company.

The bankers finally resolved to pool resources to support the stock market. When the meeting dissolved, Lamont met a swarm of reporters. "There has been a little distress selling on the Stock Exchange," he commented, "due

to a technical condition of the market." Reassuring the reporters, he added that "things were susceptible to betterment."

News of the bankers' meeting had already reached the floor of the Stock Exchange. Had the banks intervened in the market again? In anticipation, stocks steadied momentarily and even started to climb. At 1:30 P.M. the intention of the bankers' consortium became apparent. Richard Whitney, vice president of the New York Stock Exchange, was one of the best-known figures in the exchange and a floor trader for J. P. Morgan and Company. Whitney appeared on the floor of the exchange and walked over to the post where U.S. Steel was traded. Whitney started bidding at the price of the last sale, $205 for 10,000 shares. Whitney only bought 200 shares, left the rest of his order with a specialist, and moved on to the next post, placing

Anxious investors study the newspapers and call their brokers for news in this cartoon from November 1929.

On Margin.

Call Loans

During the boom of the late 1920s a large proportion of the money loaned by banks for stock purchases went into call loans. Call loans enable purchasers to buy stocks "on margin" by paying only a fraction of the purchase price of the stock—usually 45 to 50 percent, but sometimes as little as 10 percent. Buying stocks on margin works much the same way as buying a car on credit. For example, a person could buy a share of a company at $85 per share by putting up $10 of his own and borrowing $75 from his broker. If he sold the stock at $420 a year later, he would have turned his original investment of $10 into $341.25—$420 minus the broker's $75 and the 5 percent interest also owed to the broker. In this way the buyer gets the benefit of any increase in the value of the stock, but the actual value of the loan remains fixed.

In theory the lender—the brokerage house—could "call" for repayment if the stock price dropped by an amount equal to the amount borrowed. Most larger brokerage houses did not use call loans, but others used them extensively. By mid-1929 brokers had total loans outstanding of over $7 billion; in the next three months the figure grew to $8.5 billion. Interest rates for brokers' loans rocketed as high as 20 percent in March 1929.

equivalent orders for other stocks. The effect of Whitney's gesture was remarkable: Traders roared their orders again, and a boom followed. The intervention of the bankers' consortium had kept the share prices from collapsing completely. The telegraph ticker recorded the day's last transaction at 7:08 in the evening, over four hours after the end of business. It appeared that a small recovery in prices had contained the session's losses to only about a third of those of the previous day.

A TEMPORARY RECOVERY
The recovery at the end of Black Thursday was as sharp as the slump that immediately preceded it. The stock that Whitney had singled out to start the recovery—

A famous headline from Variety, *the show business paper, sums up the crash of October 29 in terms of a failed theatrical opening. Show business depended on investment to stage new productions.*

U.S. Steel—had opened at 205.5. At the lowest point of Black Thursday it was down to 193.5. It recovered to close at 206—a net gain of half a point for the day. General Electric followed a similar pattern, falling 32 points on the previous day's trading and then rising 25 points. The consortium had stemmed the chain reaction of selling brought about by the wash of securities that flooded the market. Stocks were cheap, they reasoned, and it was only a matter of time before there would be a heavy rush to buy.

Traders crowd around a ticker machine to study prices. Tickers sometimes reported price changes hours after they had happened.

CALM BEFORE THE STORM

Trading on the Stock Exchange was calmer on Friday and Saturday, but it was still heavy. Around six million shares were exchanged on Friday, and the *New York Times* Industrial Average was slightly up on the previous day's figure. Two million shares swapped hands during the short Saturday session, and the average crept downward again. Still, a general feeling of optimism pervaded the financial community. President Hoover, like Calvin Coolidge before him, felt it his duty to issue a reassuring statement, even though he had expressed his reservations about the stock-market boom in the past: "The fundamental business of the country, that is, the production and distribution of commodities, is on a sound and prosperous basis."

The Sunday newspapers forecast a better week on the stock market and urged people to purchase cut-price shares promptly. The financial community welcomed Hoover's statement, and many prominent figures shared his optimism. More astute observers did not. One such figure—then governor of New York and later U.S. president Franklin D. Roosevelt—denounced the "fever of speculation." Like other observers, he noted Hoover's implication that even though the nation's "fundamental business" might be sound, other parts of the economy were not.

Roosevelt's caution was well advised. Monday, October 28, was another disastrous day. The number of transactions was vast—some nine million shares—but not as high as on Black Thursday. Instead, it was the drop in share value that was most damaging. By the end of the day $14 billion had been lost: A remarkable three million shares changed hands in the last hour of trading. The Industrial Average was down 49 points for the day. This time it was difficult to avoid the conclusion that there was something seriously wrong.

TOTAL COLLAPSE

Unlike Black Thursday, there was no recovery. Charles E. Mitchell once again convened a meeting at J. P. Morgan and Company, and once again the market rallied. This time, however, the bankers' consortium did not support the market. They maintained their optimism that low prices would eventually stimulate trade. The market, they agreed, "retained hopeful features." The consortium met again that afternoon and reached the same conclusion. Prices would be allowed to fall.

3. BLACK TUESDAY

The next day, Black Tuesday, October 29, 1929, brought a final national collapse of share values.

million shares had been sold at a loss of $10,000,000,000 dollars. The loss was thought to be twice the amount of currency in circulation in the entire country at the time. Confusion reigned supreme, and panic beset stock exchanges across the country, including San Francisco, Los Angeles, and Chicago. Collapse seemed total.

SELL, SELL, SELL

Selling began as soon as the market opened on Tuesday morning. After only three minutes 650,000 shares of U.S. Steel, bluest of the blue-chip stocks, were dumped on the market. Such an opening came as a total surprise both to Wall Street and to exchanges across the United States, all of which were certain that the banks would step in and save the market again. But the support did not come, and traders abandoned hope that the

The losses were then the most disastrous in the history of the New York Stock Exchange. Contrary to popular belief, it was

•

"They hollered and screamed, they clawed at one another's collars."

•

not so much the small trader or speculator who suffered: Most had dropped out of the market on Black Thursday. On Black Tuesday the size of the blocks of stocks being sold indicated that it was the big institutions and investment trusts who were most involved.

Depositors eager to save their money wait for Clarke Brothers bank to open in New York after heavy withdrawals left it bankrupt.

Black Tuesday combined the worst features of Black Thursday and the previous Monday. The number of transactions was infinitely greater than on Black Thursday, and the drop in share price equaled that of Monday. When the exchange closed at 3:00 P.M., 16.4

surge of liquidations would cease. The opening quotations led to a flood of sell orders.

The volume of share traffic continued unabated. U.S. Steel fell through 200—5- to 10-point declines affected the whole stock-market listings by 10:30. By 11:00 the market was in turmoil. Great blocks of stock were dumped on the market. Values were falling 5 to 10 points in an hour. Once again the delay in the telegraphic tickers added to the confusion. To keep track of the volume of trade was impossible. Most brokerage houses abandoned all attempts to keep their quotation boards up to date.

By 1:30 P.M. confusion was replaced with near hysteria. An official from the New York Stock Exchange later described how floor traders "roared like lions and tigers. They hollered and screamed, they clawed at one another's collars." It was in the final hour of trading that the greatest damage was done. The silence of the customers' rooms, from where concerned investors

Whitney's Fall

Richard Whitney, the vice president of the stock exchange whose appearance on the trading floor calmed the panic on Black Thursday, eventually went to prison. Having lost money on his investments, he stole about $1 million to carry on investing, stealing bonds from institutions, including Harvard University, and cash from a charity fund set up to support the families of dead brokers. He went to prison for three years.

Dies Irae, *a drawing of October 29 by James Rosenberg, shows the buildings of Wall Street tumbling onto a panicking crowd.*

watched the floor, was in total contrast to the traders on the floor of the exchange itself, shouting and pushing their way through the mob to finalize their orders. Few in the customers' rooms spoke: Most just watched the frenzy until Wall Street's worst day ended.

RUMORS OF SUICIDE

As with Black Thursday, one of the features of Black Tuesday was the abundance of unfounded rumors. Legend had it that a wave of suicides followed the events on Wall Street on Tuesday. Although

the myth has proved enduring, it is inaccurate. Economist J. K. Galbraith noted in *The Great Crash, 1929*: "The number of suicides in October and November was comparatively low.... During the summer months, when the market was doing beautifully, the number of suicides was substantially higher." It was true that there were suicides in the fall—17 per

A Statistical Record

One statistical record of trading on the New York Stock Exchange is the industrial averages compiled by *The New York Times*, which have been maintained since 1911. Black Tuesday saw the greatest decline in the history of the New York Stock Exchange to that date. Shares of the best-known U.S. industrial and railroad corporations fell far below the low levels of Black Thursday. The industrial averages and the combined averages (taken from 25 representative railroad and 25 representative industrial shares) sold down to new low points for the year. The Industrial Average was down 43 points, canceling all of the gains of the previous 12 months. On September 19, 1929, the industrials were at a high of 469.49. Black Tuesday saw them drop more than 154 points to 314.95. The combined average was also at its highest value on September 19, 1929, at 311.90. The decline from that date to the low of Black Tuesday was 89.33 points to 222.57.

Dramatic losses were felt across the board:
U.S. Steel declined 17.5 points
General Electric declined 47 points
United States Industrial Alcohol declined 39.5 points
Standard Gas declined 40.5 points
Columbia Gas declined 22 points
Air Reduction declined 48 points
Allied Chemical & Dye declined 36 points
Baltimore & Ohio declined 13.375 points
A.M. Byers Company declined 30.75 points
Chesapeake & Ohio declined 23.5 points
New York Central declined 22.625 points
Westinghouse Electric declined 34.25 points
Western Union declined 39.5 points
Worthington Pump declined 29 points
Peoples Gas declined 40.5 points

These companies were the reputable and high-yield stocks on which speculation had been most frenzied: No stock could escape the waves of liquidation that characterized Black Tuesday.

100,000 of population in New York State alone. However, it seems that newspapers and public alike misinterpreted these deaths as a direct consequence of the crash.

4. AFTER THE CRASH
In the days following the biggest crash of the New York Stock Exchange many of those involved thought that the exchange should close for a period. The employees of some brokerage houses were nearing exhaustion—mistakes were increasingly common, and nerves were growing frayed. The brokerage houses urgently needed time to find out whether they were still solvent. However, such a decision could not be made lightly. If the stock exchange were to close, securities would become liable to unauthorized disposal on a "black market."

A decision to close the New York Stock Exchange could only be made by the Governing Committee of the Exchange, which was made up of about 40 members. The committee had, in fact, met at noon on Black Tuesday but had failed to come up with any sort of answer to the crisis beyond deciding to meet again later that same day. In this second meeting the committee decided that the

Ticker machines stood in offices throughout New York and elsewhere in America, feeding the bad news through to shocked investors.

stock exchange should open the next day as normal. However, it also decided to declare a series of special holidays on which the exchange would open for a limited period only.

NO ANSWER

At first the committee's decision seemed to be justified. The *New York Times* Industrial Average rose 31 points on Wednesday, October 30. The next day the exchange opened only for a short three-hour session, during which seven million shares exchanged hands. Once again the *New York Times* industrials rose another 21 points. At this point the governing

A lasting monument to the effects of the crash: A hotel, left partly built in 1929, remains unfinished in Vincennes, Indiana, a decade later.

committee decided to close the exchange for Friday, Saturday, and Sunday, although brokerage houses would be fully staffed, and the exchange floor would be open to allow traders to complete outstanding business.

The move failed to calm the trading, and Monday's market was bad. The *New York Times* industrials were down 22 points. Once again, following rumors that the banks were selling stocks, the bankers' consortium fell under scrutiny. Thomas W. Lamont faced the press to answer his critics. His answer was less than cheering: He could not explain the market dynamics.

He simply did not have an explanation as to why shares had resumed their fall. Some economists believe that the weekend break could itself have precipitated yet another plunge in share prices. Public confidence in the market was diminishing rapidly, and the additional time for investors to consider their situation over the weekend could well have led to another deluge of sell orders.

Tuesday, November 5, 1929, was election day for New York mayor, and the New York Stock Exchange therefore remained closed all day. The next day it opened for a short three-hour

session that saw a huge six million shares traded and was accompanied by another tremendous slump. The *New York Times* industrials fell 37 points, just 6 points less than the figure for Black Tuesday. Other disturbing news caused tension across the financial community: Fundamentals were also falling. The steel rate was in decline, and the commodity markets, in particular cotton and wheat, were falling sharply in the heaviest trading in weeks. This bad news continued through Thursday and Friday, leaving yet another weekend of conjecture and pessimism. Once again, Monday, November 11, was marked by a drastic decline: It continued throughout the week. The *New York Times* industrials sustained heavy losses. It seemed possible that the worst was yet to come.

BOTTOMING OUT

For the three weeks following Black Tuesday stock prices fell as dramatically as they had risen before. By mid-November roughly $26 billion had evaporated—nearly one-third of the total value of stocks just before the crash. In September 1929 industrials stood at 454; by November they were down to 229. During the next three years prices continued to drift down helplessly: In July 1932 the industrials stood at a rock bottom 58.

5. DOMESTIC CONSEQUENCES

The immediate aftermath of Black Tuesday wreaked havoc with hundreds of thousands of investors, many of whom now felt great resentment toward the financial institutions. The reputations of leaders of the financial community were ruined. Banks and brokerage houses were not to be trusted, and

Who Were the Investors?

Although there were not as many speculators on Wall Street as is sometimes thought, the three million or so Americans who lost out in the crash included a high proportion of women, even though they could not actually trade on the Stock Exchange. One paper listed "dressmakers, hairdressers, stenographers, clerks, private secretaries, department store saleswomen, milliners…even cooks and housemaids." Women owned over a third of U.S. Steel and General Motors. The Pennsylvania Railroad, of which over half was in female hands, was known on Wall Street as the "Petticoat Line."

senior figures came under official scrutiny. Business confidence evaporated, while bankruptcies and bank failures multiplied.

SCRAMBLE FOR MONEY

There was a desperate scramble for money. The stock-market crash destroyed credit: The banks seemed untrustworthy, and for obvious reasons, nobody would lend money against the value of securities. Hard currency was needed to keep businesses afloat, wages and bills paid, and bank loans maintained. Big business felt the effects, having lost vast amounts of money in the frenzied speculation leading up to the crash. The housing industry slumped as a result of a stream of foreclosures. Families lost their savings and their homes, while the profitability of industry and commerce deteriorated. Unemployment reached approximately four million in April 1930 and five million by the end of the year—accurate records were not kept until after the crash. Dole payments were nonexistent for the unemployed, and charity payments were a pittance, often as little as $3 a week for an entire family (see Volume 3, Chapter 1, "Tough in the City," and Volume 4, Chapter

5, "Welfare"). Millions of people lost everything—employment, homes, possessions. Starvation threatened the greatest food-producing country in the world.

THE CRASH AND THE DEPRESSION

One of the most frequent misinterpretations of the 1929 stock-market crash is that it was the root cause of the Great Depression. It fits accurately with a pattern that sees the boom, crash, and depression as the start, middle, and end of the same story. However, many economists find it difficult to support this theory. In his book *Great Bull Market* historian Robert Sobel categorically states: "No causal relationship between the events of late October 1929 and the Great Depression has ever been shown through the use of empirical evidence."

FREAK EVENT?

The behavior of the stock market in the months after the crash seems to confirm this theory. Although stock prices plummeted to record levels in the weeks following October 29, 1929, their values then crept back up slowly but surely. Similar recoveries have followed more recent stock-market crashes

The Fate of Charles Mitchell

At 9:00 P.M. on March 21, 1933, Assistant U.S. District Attorney Thomas E. Dewey arrested Charles E. Mitchell, chairman of the board of the National City Bank. Mitchell was charged with evasion of income taxes.

As part of his remuneration as an executive of the National City Bank, Mitchell was paid a share of the annual profits of the bank. National City enjoyed an extremely profitable 1928 and 1929: Mitchell took home $1.3 million in 1928 and a further $1.1 million in 1929. Along with other dividends and interests in numerous other activities, Mitchell faced an extremely large income tax liability. Consequently, however, Mitchell sold to his wife National City shares he had bought, making a loss on the sale amounting to well over $2 million. This effectively wrote off Mitchell's tax liability for 1929. Shortly after selling the shares, Mitchell reacquired them from his wife at the same price for which he sold them.

Much to the surprise of all concerned, not least Mitchell himself, the jury acquitted him on June 22, 1933, on the grounds that the transaction had been made in good faith. Following the decision, the government won a civil claim against the banker. Mitchell was ordered to pay $1.1 million in overdue taxes and charges. After an appeal to the U.S. Supreme Court he finally settled with the government on December 27, 1938.

A newspaper seller on Wall Street. Papers reported the effects of the crash at the same time as they issued calls for calm.

(see box, page 101). By April 1930 the market had recouped about 20 percent of the losses of the previous October. The *New York Times* Industrial Average stood at the same level it had been at the start of 1929, and the country's major financial institutions were still operating steadily.

Another persistent misconception about the crash is that it drastically affected many smaller investors, a version of events reinforced by the popular writer Frederick Lewis Allen in his 1931 essay "Only Yesterday." An estimate by the New York Stock Exchange in 1929 counted some 20 million

The Dot.com Phenomenon

The collapse of share values for new-technology companies in 2000 prompted comparisons with previous catastrophic collapses on stock markets worldwide, including the Great Crash. The stock prices of the so-called dot.com companies fell sharply. Could the collapse have heralded a global economic disaster? Most experts think not. Since many of the new Internet companies run at a loss, their stocks are far more vulnerable to wild swings in price than traditional stocks. Often the share price reflects demand for the stock rather than its intrinsic value. In such developing sectors investors tend to trade more speculatively and more frequently than in normal shares, dipping in and out of the market. This makes the price vulnerable to changes in opinion. Spring 2000 saw a fall in the values of new-technology stocks and a return to more traditional old-economy companies. Share prices in such companies had fallen as investors rushed to buy new-economy shares but now recovered.

Automobiles stand in the empty showrooms of the Washington-Cadillac Company in Washington, D.C. Slow sales, caused initially by overproduction, were worsened by the effects of the Great Crash.

U.S. citizens as owning stocks. In fact, probably only about three million people—less than 2.5 percent of the population—owned stocks and shares. Even indirect ownership of securities was minimal, since today's situation in which pension funds invest in the stock market, thus involving all their investors in the market, did not exist. The crash had little direct effect on the average U.S. citizen.

6. WORLDWIDE REPERCUSSIONS

The Great Crash and its aftermath precipitated an economic collapse around the world. During the 1920s the United States had been the only industrial nation not crippled by World War I (1914–1918). It was the only source of money available to those nations that owed war debts and to Germany, which had to make vast reparations payments to the Allies. However, U.S. banks had realized that it was more profitable to invest in stocks and shares rather than lend to overseas nations, whose debts remained unpaid.

The events of 1929 left such countries no longer able to depend on the United States for financial assistance or trade; they could not repay their postwar loans. The United States, meanwhile, was unable to afford imports from the rest of the world.

As it had often done in the past, the United States fell back on protectionism, using high tariffs to discourage imports and encourage domestic industry. This protectionism, in the form of the Smoot-Hawley Tariff of 1930, had a disastrous effect on the failing economies of nations like Great Britain and France. All these factors depressed world trade and began the deep depression that would badly affect the international economy in the 1930s.

History Repeating?

The New York Stock Exchange has experienced a number of difficulties since it first opened for trading back in 1817. One of the first recorded slumps occurred on September 18, 1873, when the firm Jay Cooke and Company failed, resulting in the collapse of 57 other stock exchange firms in the following weeks. A far more recent example is Black Monday, which occurred on October 19, 1987. Black Monday was marked by stock-market prices that fell through the floor, precipitating the collapse of all the major stock markets, including London and Tokyo. The Dow Jones Industrial Average fell some 500 points, wiping over 22 percent off the value of securities.

The 1987 crash was the culmination of months of severe declines in the bond market. October had also seen three days of rapidly declining share values before Black Monday's total collapse. Economists laid the blame on underlying weaknesses in the U.S. economy and Wall Street's computer systems, which automatically triggered an avalanche of sell orders when prices reached a certain low point on the day. However, the financial crisis eased in the week following Black Monday, and by the end of 1987 the Dow Jones Industrial Average had recovered its previous value.

Why did Black Monday not trigger a worldwide economic crisis of the magnitude that was seen in the months following Black Tuesday 1929? In many ways today's stock market is subject to a number of strict government measures and controls, quite unlike the stock market of 1929. For example, the U.S. Federal Reserve System has been strengthened to retain measures of responsibility over individual Reserve banks and other member banks. Margin requirements can be set to avoid exorbitant interest rates, and the stock market is also subject to regulation through various commissions.

The precise cause of the total collapse that followed the crash of 1929 remains a topic of debate in economic circles. However, the uneven distribution of income, poor corporate structure, poor banking structure, the dubious state of the foreign balance, and the poor state of economic information all seemed to have played a part in creating an inherently weak economy. The economy at the time of subsequent crashes, such as in 1987, was in nothing like such a fragile condition.

7

HOOVER: THE SEARCH FOR A SOLUTION

Herbert Clark Hoover won the 1928 U.S. presidential election on the strength of his reputation as the best man to influence the business cycle and thereby sustain economic growth at the levels to which Americans had become accustomed during the Roaring Twenties. But the crisis that soon engulfed the United States was beyond his control.

A farm for sale in the Midwest. Farm sales and mortgage foreclosures were characteristic of Hoover's early presidency.

It was to some extent bad luck for Herbert Hoover that he should succeed Coolidge just as the Depression started to bite (see Chapter 5, "The Fantasy World"). He won the election in November 1928 and was sworn in on March 4, 1929. Seven months

•

"It was Hoover who got its blast, and was fried, boiled, roasted, and fricasseed."

•

later came the Wall Street crash (see Chapter 6, "The Crash of 1929"). Hoover became inextricably linked with the Depression because of his failure to cope with

Herbert Hoover (right) with his predecessor, Calvin Coolidge. Neither favored federal intervention in the economy, placing them in a long tradition of self-reliance and the free market.

its extent, and observers sometimes came to the conclusion that he was somehow its author, or was at least to blame for making it worse. H. L. Mencken (1880–1956; see box, page 57) was nearer the truth when he wrote that there had been "a volcano boiling under Coolidge. When it burst forth at last, it was Hoover who got its blast, and was fried, boiled, roasted, and fricasseed."

When Hoover took office, expectations were high. Business seemed solid, and incomes were rising. His campaign slogan promised a "new day." In his inauguration address he said, "I have no fears for the future of our country. It is bright with hope."

Hoover seemed the ideal choice for president. A Quaker from West Branch, Iowa, who believed passionately in peace, he had studied mining engineering at Stanford University and then made a fortune from mine and railroad construction before devoting his time to selfless endeavor for the welfare of others.

1. THE GREAT ENGINEER

When the United States entered World War I in April 1917, Hoover was called to Washington to serve as food administrator (see Chapter 2, "The United States in World War I"). The office was created to encourage agricultural production and food conservation and to coordinate fair distribution of available resources. When the war ended in November 1918, Woodrow Wilson sent Hoover to Europe to direct the American Relief Administration, set up to alleviate suffering caused by the war's destruction. The ARA fed 10 million people and provided funds for the postwar reconstruction of Belgium.

Back home, such activities raised Hoover's popularity to the extent that some people hoped he would run for the presidency in 1920. Previously he had never participated in party politics; but while refusing to seek election that year, he did declare himself a Republican. In 1921 President Warren G. Harding appointed Hoover secretary of commerce. Even while the United States retreated further into isolationism, withdrawing itself from the affairs of Europe (see Chapter 3, "The Return to Normalcy"), Hoover extended aid to the Soviet Union when it was stricken by famine after the 1917 Communist revolution. When a critic inquired if he was not helping Bolshevism, Hoover replied, "Twenty million people are starving. Whatever their politics, they shall be fed."

Hoover was widely seen as the chief architect of Republican prosperity and had impressive credentials as a politician in the progressive tradition, advocating social reform through political moderation. He enjoyed a high reputation as a principled humanitarian. Throughout his political career from 1914 to his death in 1964 Hoover did not take any pay: He gave all his presidential salary to charity. His only apparent

A combine harvester working in a barley field in 1929. The price of grain began to fall that year and kept falling over the next four years. Farmers who had gone into debt to buy new machinery were among those worse hit by the financial crash.

shortcoming was shyness, which made him a poor orator. He found speaking to crowds an ordeal and came across as stiff and dull.

Soon after taking office, Hoover convened a special session of Congress to deal with the struggling agricultural sector (see Volume 3, Chapter 2, "Shadow over the Countryside"). Although his proposals for revising agricultural tariffs got tangled in detail and had to be carried over to the regular Congressional session, he pushed through the Agricultural Marketing Act, which established the Federal Farm Board. With an initial sum of $500 million the board was to provide technical and promotional assistance to farmers, make loans to facilitate orderly marketing, and form emergency stabilization corporations to deal with demoralized markets.

Women and children, victims of the drought that hit in 1930, stand forlornly outside their ramshackle house in Arkansas.

INCREASED TARIFFS

Hoover originally proposed higher tariffs on imported farm products, a move intended to open up stagnant markets. After 14 months of struggle with competing interests in Congress, however, he settled for a general upward revision of tariffs on manufactured goods as well as farm produce.

The most significant—and ultimately the most damaging—of the tariff revision measures was the bill brought before Congress in June 1930 by Senator Reed Smoot of Utah and Oregon congressman Willis Hawley. The Smoot-Hawley

Act (see box, page 107) raised import duties on many foreign products to a record average of 60 percent. It was intended to protect U.S. businesses from foreign competition and so help reduce the growing unemployment rate. More than 1,000 economists petitioned Hoover to veto the bill because, they predicted, it would raise prices to consumers, damage export trade, promote inefficiency, provoke foreign reprisals, and ultimately hurt the farmers it had been intended to help.

Hoover felt that he had to follow the wishes of his party in a Congressional election year. The critics of the act were proved right, however. More than 60 of the United States' trading partners retaliated with higher tariffs of their own, and largely as a result world trade declined rapidly. By stifling international trade, the Smoot-Hawley Act would contribute significantly to the length and severity of the Great Depression.

OTHER REFORMS

Hoover's early initiatives were complemented by reforms in other areas. The administration rationalized veterans' benefits, for instance, strengthened its relations with labor by endorsing a broad view of employers' responsibilities, and undertook some prison reform. It attempted to depoliticize the Prohibition enforcement agencies and organized a major fact-finding commission to study law and order. Hoover overrode the objections of Treasury Secretary Andrew W. Mellon (1855–1937) and announced a plan for tax reductions on low incomes.

On a personal level Hoover shunned corrupt patronage and would not tolerate "red hunts" or

The furnaces of the Tennessee Coal Iron and Railroad Company in Ensley, Alabama. Single-industry communities could be devastated by a market collapse.

interference with peaceful picketing of the White House. He defended his wife's decision to invite to the White House Mrs. Oscar De Priest, the wife of Chicago's new African American congressman, and also sought more money for the all-black Howard University.

STOCK-MARKET CRASH

The concealed volcano to which Mencken referred blew its top on Wall Street. On September 4, 1929, stock prices wavered and the next day dropped. In October the value of stocks on the New York Exchange fell by a huge average of 37 percent in a series of spectacular collapses. Business and government leaders still expressed hope for the economic future, however, some because they really believed that the prospects for recovery were good, others because they believed that it was their obligation as leaders to make optimistic statements. According to Hoover himself, "the fundamental business of the country" remained sound.

Some speculators who got out of the market went back in for bargains but found themselves caught up in the erosion of stock values. Consumers and business leaders proceeded with extreme caution. Buyers held out for lower prices, orders fell off, wages plummeted or ceased to be paid altogether, and the decline in purchasing power brought further cutbacks in business activity. From 1929 to 1932 Americans' personal incomes declined by more than half, from $82 million to $40

million. Unemployment rose rapidly, from 1.6 million in 1929 to 12.8 million in 1933, from 3 percent to 25 percent of the workforce. Farmers faced disaster as commodity prices fell by half, and thousands of farms had to be sold to pay off their debts. More than 9,000 local banks closed during the period, and hundreds of factories and mines were shut down; sometimes entire towns were abandoned.

2. HOOVER'S RESPONSE TO THE CRASH

The collapse of the stock market finally revealed the flimsy foundations on which the "get-rich-quick" economy had been built. During the boom years of the mid-1920s too many businesses maintained prices and raised profits by holding down wages, with the result that one-third of personal income now went to only one-twentieth of the population.

Businesses used their profits to finance expansion, creating a growing imbalance between rising productivity and declining purchasing power. As the demand for goods fell, the rate of investment in new plants and equipment tailed off. For a time the decline in purchasing power was concealed by greater use of installment buying, where consumers paid for items in a series of small payments over a set period. The deflationary effects of high tariffs were hidden by the volume of loans and investments abroad, which helped maintain foreign demand for U.S. goods. But as soon as the domestic stock market began to seem a more attractive investment, the flow of American

Herbert Hoover signing the Farm Relief Bill in June 1929. The bill came too late to help stricken farmers, many of whom lost their farms to the mortgage holders.

The Smoot-Hawley Tariff

During the early 1900s many people in the United States wanted to stimulate the nation's businesses by lowering the tariffs on imported goods: Such tariffs were intended to protect American jobs from overseas competition by making imports cost more than domestic goods. The Payne-Aldrich Tariff of 1909 changed many tariff rates but did not greatly reduce their average level. In 1913 the Underwood Tariff Act lowered tariffs more significantly, but in 1922 the Fordney-McCumber Tariff Act reversed the trend and raised rates sharply again.

During the 1920s, when it practiced a policy of isolationism from world affairs, the United States remained largely in favor of tariffs. In 1930 this attitude reached its highpoint in the Smoot-Hawley Tariff. The tariff raised import duties so significantly—by an average of 60 percent—that many historians believe it played a major part in the decline in the world economy. The tariff stirred hostility abroad and reduced the ability of European countries to pay war debts to the United States.

The Smoot-Hawley Tariff was largely an answer to the crisis in agriculture in the United States and largely concerned farm commodities. Many politicians and economists protested against the tariff, fearful that it would have a negative effect on world trade. Despite their opposition the act became law. One section of the law prohibited the importation, after January 1, 1932, of goods produced by convict, forced, or indentured labor. Forced labor was defined as "all work or service which is exacted from any person under the menace of penalty for its nonperformance and for which the worker does not offer himself voluntarily." This might be interpreted as banning goods produced under certain communist or fascist governments.

As its critics had warned, the tariff was greeted by hostility in Europe. The higher import duties placed a new burden on countries that were already in debt to the United States. Because duties made their goods too expensive to sell in the United States, they had to pay their debts with larger payments of cash, of which they were in short supply.

---

capital overseas was reduced to a trickle. The rich were enticed into market speculation by the prospect of swollen profits and dividends. As soon as there was trouble, confidence vanished and the bottom fell out of the market.

HOOVER'S PHILOSOPHY

Many Americans who had suffered in the crash looked to the government for help. Hoover's response has often been portrayed—not least by members of the Roosevelt administration that succeeded him—as being woefully complacent. His critics accuse him of essentially doing nothing as the Depression worsened. In fact, Hoover's response to the crisis was nothing like as clear-cut.

Hoover was a passionate believer in the freedom and enterprise of the individual and therefore the limitation of federal power. One of the central tenets of his beliefs—called Hooverism— was that rather than adopting regulation and coercion, the government should concentrate on putting in place the right economic infrastructure, which would then benefit everyone.

Hoover's attitude was echoed by most politicians and economists, who initially refused to acknowledge the severity of the crisis. All that was needed, they thought, was a slight correction of the market. The majority of policymakers who subscribed to the economic theory of laissez-faire, or

no government intervention in business, clung firmly to the belief that the economy would cure itself. Previous financial panics and depressions had all been reversed in just a year or two.

Like many others, Hoover still believed that the U.S. economy was basically sound. He believed that the maintenance of price levels and continued spending would bring economic recovery. In 1930 few people expected the slump to continue. The situation this time was different, however. Mass production had eliminated more industrial jobs than it had created, while the supply of goods continued to exceed demand. At the same time, the world market was basically unsound. European

Hoover attending a conference on unemployment. Rather than intervene in the labor market, he believed his role was to create the circumstances in which unions and employers could work out the best solutions for both sides.

countries, in particular, had been badly hit by the slump. Its negative effect on their economies, which were still recovering after World War I, left them unable to pay their international debts. This in turn would have severe repercussions for the U.S. economy.

In his inaugural address in March Hoover had affirmed his commitment to free enterprise and minimal government interference: "The election has again confirmed the determination of the American people that regulation of private enterprise and not government ownership or operation is the course rightly to be pursued in our relation to business." After the crash he publicly maintained this attitude, remarking, "Prosperity cannot be restored by raids upon the public treasury."

Hoover tried to instill optimism in the economy by downplaying the depth of the crisis. He was anxious that influential politicians and business leaders should also give out upbeat messages. Critics mocked what they saw as a head-in-sand attitude. Even one Republican senator observed wryly, "Every time an adminis-

tration official gives out an optimistic statement about business conditions the market immediately drops."

REACTION TO THE CRASH

Hoover refused to abandon his philosophy completely in the face of the crisis. He still insisted that there should be strict limits on action by the federal government.

However, he also took some measures to alleviate the problems. This was a paradox of Hoover's administration: His intellectual certainty that federal intervention was wrong often conflicted with his pragmatic recognition that it was needed in the present emergency. After the Wall Street Crash he announced that he would cut taxes in order to increase spending power and expand public works' spending to encourage employment. He still insisted, however, on the importance of keeping the federal budget balanced: He would not

A Hooverville outside a factory: When workers lost their homes, building such shelters was one of the few remedies open to them.

go into debt to spend his way out of depression.

Hoover, who was sometimes known as the Great Engineer, preferred to involve himself in the economy as a communicator and facilitator, bringing sides together or applying pressure to achieve a certain resolution. In order to protect purchasing power, for example, he sought to ensure that companies would allow their profits to fall rather than cut wages. He called business and labor leaders together and proposed that they keep their factories and shops open, maintain wage levels, and spread work to avoid layoffs. In return he got union leaders to agree to refrain from high wage demands and strikes. They did this on the whole reluctantly, but they had little choice.

THINGS GET WORSE

Events were now outstripping the most carefully drafted legislation of a fundamentally noninterventionist government. As business failures increased and unemployment and debt soared, it became clear that the country was in the grip of economic breakdown.

Some of the problems were exacerbated by traditional weaknesses in the U.S. economy. The lax enforcement of antitrust laws encouraged anticompetitive practices like concentration and monopoly, which encouraged businesses to maintain high prices. Hostility toward unions discouraged collective bargaining; the wages of rich and poor grew even further apart.

In the economic uncertainty, meanwhile, some of Hoover's policies did not have the desired effects. The tax reductions encouraged people to save rather than spend, reducing even further the demand for consumer goods. When he ordered the Federal Reserve to provide easier credit to increase people's purchasing power, the increase in the money supply and reduced interest rates

Supply and Demand

Hoover, like other supporters of classical or laissez-faire economic theory, believed that an economy worked most efficiently when government left it alone. Classical theory, as formulated in the 18th century by the British economist Adam Smith, proposed that an economy was subject to certain natural laws that regulated its operations (see Volume 4, Chapter 1, "Left vs. Right"). One of the most important of those laws was that of supply and demand; most modern countries work on the basis of a supply-and-demand market economy.

The theory of supply and demand tries to explain the actions of both consumers and producers: Members of society demand certain goods in order to live at a certain level, and other members of society supply them. Supply and demand dictates what goods are produced and what they cost. The supply of a particular good depends on what price producers think they can charge for it: If they cannot cover their costs, or make a healthy profit, they will not make the good. The demand for a product also varies. The market may only want a certain number of cars. If the producer makes more, he will have to lower his prices to create more demand; if he produces too few, the price will rise as consumers outbid each other. An ideal free-market economy would be self-regulating: Prices would rise and fall to balance supply and demand. If demand is higher than supply, the price of goods will rise; if supply is greater, the price will fall.

One of the reasons Hoover failed to react more rapidly when the Depression hit was that he, like many others, believed that the laws of supply and demand would operate to stabilize the economy. After the rise in production throughout the 1920s the supply of many goods far outstripped any demand for them; manufacturers were left with stockpiled goods, and prices tumbled.

According to classical theory, the lower prices should have stimulated demand. What actually happened was that manufacturers' profits fell; they responded by cutting wages or firing workers. The people who in theory should have been buying the cheaper goods either had so little money or were so worried about their financial security that they did not buy them. Supply-and-demand theory had proved unreliable; during the Great Depression economists and politicians would seek new ways to understand how modern economies work.

only encouraged speculation as investors tried to make their money earn more interest. The

•

"Prosperity cannot be restored by raids upon the public treasury."

•

increased federal spending on public works' projects to create employment was negated by cutbacks in state and local funding for similar projects. The Smoot-Hawley Tariff devastated foreign trade.

3. THE WORSENING CRISIS

The beleaguered agricultural sector suffered another blow in August 1930 when drought struck the Plains states: A million farmers watched their crops die. Hoover expected that the crisis would be relieved by local aid from municipalities, but the funding the farmers received from such sources was insufficient; a few months later an outcry demanded federal intervention. Hoover, who believed that people should only be helped to help themselves, refused aid because, like many other Americans of the time, he thought it would undermine moral fiber (see Volume 4, Chapter 5, "Welfare"). He refused to support a bill to give the Red Cross millions of dollars, for example, because he said it did not need the money. When he did support an act that provided farmers with money to buy food for livestock, his political enemies wondered why he thought it wise to feed starving cattle but wicked to feed starving men and women.

The Red Cross took truckloads of cornmeal to people living in isolated communities. Hoover maintained that such private charity was the best way to cope with the crisis.

Hoover personally bore the brunt of the blame for the Great Depression, and his support among voters quickly eroded. Near city dumps and along railroad tracks the bankrupt and homeless huddled in their "Hooverville" shacks made of tar paper, corrugated iron, and old packing boxes. In 1930 the Democrats gained their first national victory since 1916, winning a majority in the House of Representatives.

FALSE DAWN

In the first half of 1931 economic indicators rose. It seemed for a while as if Hoover might have been right to believe that the economy would correct itself, but then another shock jolted public confidence. Although it was set off by German, Austrian, and French actions, it was the repercussion of U.S. policy that had been responsible for the creation of an international monetary system that depended on a continued outflow of capital from the United States.

EUROPEAN BANK FAILURE

In March 1931 German chancellor Heinrich Bruning, in an attempt to bolster his country's economy and thus make Adolf Hitler less attractive to voters, proposed a customs union with Austria. The move was blocked by France, which feared that it would lead to the German annexation of Austria. The French reaction made it increasingly difficult for Austria's overextended banking system to obtain funds.

When in early May it became public that one of the country's most important banks, Louis Rothschild's Kreditanstalt in Vienna, had received special

Confidence

Hoover believed that the country's greatest need was confidence. Again and again he exhorted the American public to keep up hope. On May 1, 1930, for example, he boldly told the U.S. Chamber of Commerce, "We have passed the worst and with continued effort we shall rapidly recover."

government support to stay open, there was a run on the bank as investors tried to withdraw their money. The bank had to close. Panic liquidation followed as people tried to turn their savings and investments into cash and gold. The next two months brought a domino effect of exchange crises and runs on banks throughout central and western Europe. Gold flowed out of Germany and Austria.

Reparation Problems

One of the main causes of the European crisis was the reparations Germany had been ordered to pay by the Treaty of Versailles (see box, page 113). Germany's postwar need for reconstruction and restrictions on its economic activity meant that it could not generate money to pay its debts. Hoover proposed to break this vicious circle by means of new international initiatives. Although he had always been committed to balancing the budget, he now saw that other economic priorities were more pressing. In the cabinet he likened the economic crisis to a war, saying: "In war times, no one dreamed of balancing the budget. Fortunately we can borrow."

On June 5, 1931, Hoover proposed a one-year moratorium on intergovernment debts—what governments owed to one another, including Germany's reparations

Shacks in this Hooverville on the Willamette River in Portland, Oregon, offered minimal comfort to their occupants.

payments—and later a temporary standstill on the settlement of private obligations between banks. The move aimed to give Germany breathing space and the world economy chance to recover.

Hoover's proposal was enlightened self-interest. The European crisis had brought new downturns in the U.S. economy. American businesses welcomed the plan, figuring that the more economically stable and less indebted Germany and other European states were, the better their prospects of being paid by firms there.

The Gold Standard

The moratorium took effect on July 6, 1931. The major European nations accepted it, but it helped create a shortage of monetary exchange by slowing the international circulation of money. This led Europeans to withdraw their gold from American banks and dispose of their American securities. One by one the European nations devalued their currencies.

European nations also abandoned the gold standard, the instrument by which countries pegged the exchange rate of their currencies to the price of gold and the amount of it they held in their reserves. A country that was losing gold was supposed to deflate its economy, reducing prices to stimulate exports, and raise interest rates to attract foreign investment and thus arrest the outflow of capital. Although this worked well in theory and in times of prosperity, it did not work in the current crisis. In 1931 the United States slid into a third winter of depression and, for many, hopelessness.

4. HOOVER INITIATIVES

In the United States, powerful liberals began to take independent action, following the lead of Governor Franklin D. Roosevelt (1882–1945). Roosevelt, in the fall of 1931, established a state emergency relief administration in New York. With a new Congress in session, increased demands for federal action now impelled Hoover to stretch his philosophy of government to the limit. He finally accepted the need to use governmental resources to shore up the nation's financial institutions and called for tax increases to balance the federal budget. To this end he submitted to Congress a bill that became the Tax Revenue Act of 1932. Despite creating half a million new taxpayers, and thus increased tax receipts, the legislation failed to balance the federal budget, which ended the year $2.7 billion in the red.

A poster from 1931 encourages people to use gas in order to stimulate work for miners.

German Reparations

At the end of World War I Germany got the blame for starting the conflict and therefore made to pay for much of the damage the country had caused to other nations by what were called reparations. This meant paying back huge amounts of money, which for a country already in economic crisis was difficult. In 1921, for instance, Germany's inability to give a satisfactory response to demands for reparations led to British, French, and Belgian troops crossing the Rhine River and occupying Dusseldorf and other towns.

Another plan, originated in Britain but not implemented, intended to force the Germans to pay financial penalties on their exports. Every purchaser of German goods would have to give a proportion, say 50 percent, of the purchase money to the Treasury; the German exporter would then have to apply to his government for reimbursement. Businessmen were skeptical, though, believing the Germans would get around this by trading through neutral countries. Germany accepted the principle of reparations but said it could only pay a quarter of the $10 billion the Allies demanded.

Ten years later the problem had not gone away. Indeed, it was now affecting the world economy. In 1931 Herbert Hoover proposed that all war debts should be suspended for one year in an effort to get the world economy out of its slump. In the meantime Germany had worked out a trade pact with Austria to try to help its worsening economic condition. The deal was blocked; and Austria, which like Germany was losing its gold to the United States, suffered. When it was learned that the Rothschild bank, Kreditanstalt, had been given special government support, there was run on the bank, and it had to close its doors.

With banks closing and Germany's gold reserves running out, the situation reached crisis point. The German currency, the mark, collapsed, and Allied leaders had to agree to renew credits for Germany for up to three months. The settlements would have to be reworked yet again.

The economic and political situation in Europe was now in turmoil, and that, in turn, had a negative effect on the economic crisis in America. Reparations, it seems, had caused more harm than good.

Crisis Policies

Hoover again responded to the deepening crisis, but history has been unkind in its assessment of the wisdom of his actions. The Glass-Steagall Act liberalized Federal Reserve credit policy to inject cash into the economy; it also provided $750 million of gold to meet the foreign withdrawals. The 1932 Federal Home Loan Bank Act aimed to strengthen the real estate market by creating savings-and-loan associations. Also enacted in 1932 were a surplus disposal law, which authorized the Farm Board to hand farm produce to the Red Cross for distribution to the needy, a revenue act to increase federal finances and allay fears about the soundness of government credit, and an economy act cutting federal salaries and services and authorizing administrative reorganization to save money.

THE RECONSTRUCTION FINANCE CORPORATION

One of Hoover's most important measures against rising unemployment came in January 1932 with the creation of the Reconstruction Finance Corporation (RFC). The corporation was given $500 million—and authority to borrow $1.5 billion more—to make emergency loans to banks, life insurance companies, building and loan societies, farm mortgage associations, and railroads. This action went against Hoover's deeply held beliefs that private initiative was more desirable than state intervention, that the charity of the haves would "trickle down" to benefit the have-nots, and that welfare would weaken both the economy and people's will to work. The RFC was effective at staving off some bankruptcies, but critics charged that it favored business owners at the expense of labor and the workers.

STIMULATING LOCAL GOVERNMENT

Hoover also tried to stimulate local and charitable assistance to the needy, first through the

President's Emergency Committee for Employment and, from 1932, through its successor, the President's Organization for Unemployment Relief. The sums raised by these bodies were substantial but inadequate. The total collected in a year in New York—$79 million—was less than the wages lost in a month by the city's unemployed. When the head of the charity, Walter S. Gifford, was questioned by a Senate committee, he admitted that he did not even know how many people were out of work or drawing relief, nor how much money his organization had raised.

"TRICKLE DOWN" PRINCIPLE
Hoover's critics argued that federal measures relied on the same "trickle down" principle as his charitable foundations. "If government could help banks and railroads," asked Senator Robert F. Wagner (1877–1953), "is there any reason why we should not likewise extend a helping hand to that forlorn American, in every

•

"... the doors of revolt in this country are going to be thrown open."

•

village and every city of the United States, who has been without wages since 1929?"

The contraction of credit had had a devastating effect on farmers and other debtors who had made purchases on installment plans or who held balloon mortgages, the monthly payments on which increased over time. Members of Congress, conscious that previous efforts to pull out of depression were inadequate, proposed bill after bill to provide federal relief for distressed individuals.

Hoover, the great humanitarian, was now widely perceived as uncaring. On July 21, 1932, however, he signed the Emergency Relief and Construction Act, which avoided a direct federal dole but gave the RFC $300 million for relief loans to the states, authorized loans of up to $1.5 billion for state and local government con-

Red Cross workers donate citrus fruit to the drought-stricken farmers in Mississippi.

Feeding the Poor

Among the groups who helped to feed the needy during the Great Depression was the American Red Cross. It began as the American Association for the Relief of Misery on the Battlefields and adopted the red cross as its emblem. This group disbanded in 1871, however, because the United States had not yet ratified the Geneva Convention, an international agreement that set out the rules of behavior during war and under which the Red Cross operated.

Clara Barton worked to have the treaty ratified and subsequently helped establish the American Association of the Red Cross in 1881. President Chester A. Arthur finally signed the treaty on March 1, 1882. The Red Cross association was then reorganized, and in 1905 Congress granted a new charter that established the organization of the American Red Cross more or less as it is today. During World War I the Red Cross grew in numbers and worked to meet the welfare needs of soldiers who fought in the war. In 1917 it set up Home Service facilities to provide a link between soldiers and their families. It also equipped 58 base hospitals, mostly abroad.

After the war the Red Cross helped millions of veterans and during the 1920s established 2,400 public health nursing services around the U.S. When the depression hit, the Red Cross took on the role of helping feed the poor. Its trucks carried much needed supplies into remote areas and made sure needy families received fruit and other essential foodstuffs, often donated from elsewhere. This help was essential for many farmers whose farms had failed, and who had no means of support.

struction projects, and appropriated $322 million for federal public works.

CHAOS AND REVOLUTION

Meanwhile, the government had virtually given up attempting to provide relief for farmers. In mid-1931 it quit buying surplus produce and let prices slide. The effect was devastating. The price of virtually every crop fell year after year for four years from 1929. In 1919 wheat had fetched $2.16 a bushel; by 1932 it had sunk to 38 cents. Cotton had reached a high of 41.75 cents a pound in 1919; before the 1932 harvest it fell to 4.6 cents. Other farm prices declined comparably. Between 1930 and 1934 the titles of nearly a million farms passed from their owners to mortgage holders who foreclosed on the loans.

Faced with total loss, some desperate farmers began to defy the law. Angry mobs stopped foreclosures and threatened to lynch bankers and judges. In Nebraska farmers burned corn to keep warm, while dairy farmers poured

•

"I am so tired… that every bone in my body aches."

•

milk into roadside ditches in an effort to raise prices. Most of these strikes failed, but they achieved widespread publicity for the farmers' cause. Some people feared that they represented the seeds of a communist revolution. One labor leader warned: "If something is not done and starvation is going to continue, the doors of revolt in this country are going to be thrown open."

Hoover had worked hard to deliver his country from the grip of the Great Depression, but he knew that he had failed. "I am so tired," he said, "that every bone in my body aches." Presidential news briefings became more strained and less frequent. When friends urged Hoover to assert himself and lead from the front, he replied, "I can't be a Theodore Roosevelt" or "I have no Wilsonian qualities." His gloom and growing sense of futility communicated themselves to a depressed nation.

HOOVER'S CONTRIBUTION

Despite the many failures of his policies, Hoover had planted many seeds that would bear fruit in the years to come. The banking legislation of Roosevelt's New

Deal had largely been drawn up under Hoover. He planned the Grand Coulee Dam in Washington state and flood relief measures along the Mississippi. He signed a treaty with Canada to create the St. Lawrence Waterway. His administration increased the acreage of national forests and parks by 5 million acres. The airmail service was reorganized, and passenger service tripled. Hoover used RFC funds to build the San Francisco Bay Bridge. He drew up legislation to protect children and wrote a Children's Charter calling for the protection of the rights of every child regardless of race or situation.

A bulldozer works on a road beside the San Francisco Bay Bridge in this 1938 photograph.

Hoover had also made reforms in judicial procedures and bankruptcy practice to help small businesses and homeowners. He had reorganized the FBI under J. Edgar Hoover (see Volume 3, Chapter 5, "Crime in the Depression"), planned an extensive reform of criminal justice, and made three high-caliber appointments to the U.S. Supreme Court: Chief Justice Charles Evans Hughes and justices Owen Roberts and Benjamin Cardozo (see Volume 4, Chapter 2, "The Supreme Court"). In foreign affairs he led the United States to greater international cooperation with the Hoover-Stimson Doctrine, which stated that the U.S. would not recognize territories gained by force. He developed a Good Neighbor policy with Latin America and withdrew U.S. troops

from Nicaragua and Haiti. He made a breakthrough at the London Naval Conference in 1930 by persuading Britain and Japan to become cosignatories with the United States of a treaty limiting the buildup of warships that took account of a navy's age, armaments, and fighting strength.

But millions of poor and hungry Americans were convinced that Hoover's sense of history would neither find them work nor put food on their tables; his presidency had prescribed treatment for the symptoms of the Depression while the disease ran unchecked through the body of American life. They wanted action and they wanted it right away. They firmly believed that Franklin Roosevelt was the person who could give it to them.

The Bonus Army

Veterans relax on the Capitol lawn as they wait for news of the vote on their bonus payment.

One of the defining incidents of Hoover's presidency came in summer 1932, when around 10,000 veterans of World War I and their families—around 20,000 people in all—descended on Washington, D.C. The so-called Bonus Expeditionary Force laid siege to the Capitol to protest against the delay in paying the $1,000 war-service bonus they had been promised. They camped on the lawns and marched around the building in what they called the "death march," which went on day and night. Many set up home in a shantytown in Anacostia, across the Potomac River; others lived in encampments downtown. Hoover refused to meet the protesters but asked the police to provide them with beds and Army food.

The House of Representatives had offered the veterans a cash payment of $500, but Hoover threatened to stop it. Given the financial crisis, he argued, the state could not afford the payment without unbalancing the budget. On June 17, 1932, the Senate backed the president: The 3.5 million ex-servicemen would have to wait for their bonus until 1945. At the news the men sang "America" and went back to their camps. Hoover decided that they must be dispersed in case they became a mob.

Hoover's negotiators, Secretary of War Patrick Hurley and General Douglas MacArthur, had little sympathy with the protesters, whom they saw as dangerous communists. When talks broke down, the police and troops moved in to clear the downtown encampments. Although Hoover had forbidden violence, cavalrymen charged the veterans. The infantry followed with tear gas and set fire to the camp. Again disobeying Hoover, MacArthur crossed the Potomac and gassed and burned the main camp at Anacostia (below). Two babies died from the gas before the veterans and their families fled.

Hoover was trapped: He disapproved of MacArthur's actions but could not be seen to support people he believed were subversives. He later repeated MacArthur's false claim that only 10 percent of the protesters were real veterans: The real figure was closer to 95 percent. There was little evidence of communist influence at Anacostia. MacArthur had deliberately disobeyed the head of the government and gone unpunished for it.

GLOSSARY

balanced budget an economic term used to describe a situation in which a government's income is enough to pay for all its expenditure. The balanced budget was an essential principle in U.S. economic policy until Roosevelt adopted deficit spending in 1937. *See also* deficit spending.

business cycle an economic term used to describe the periodic but unpredictable and inexplicable rise and fall of economic activity.

capitalism an economic system in which private individuals and companies control the production and distribution of goods and services.

communism a political doctrine advocated by Karl Marx and Friedrich Engels in the 19th century that proposes the overthrow of capitalism and its replacement by working-class rule. Communism was the official ideology of the Soviet Union and was highly feared in the United States.

deficit spending an economic approach in which a government goes into debt in order to fund its activities. Deficit spending is a central tenet of Keynesianism.

depression a deep trough in the business cycle. No other depression matched the intensity of or lasted as long as the Great Depression.

fascism a political ideology based on authoritarian rule and suppression, aggressive nationalism, and militarism.

gold standard an economic tool that used gold as the measure of a nation's currency, so that one unit of currency always bought a fixed amount of gold. It was chiefly useful in stabilizing exchange rates between currencies.

Hundred Days the name given to Roosevelt's first period as president, from March 9 to June 16, 1933, characterized by a whirl of legislative activity. It was named for the Hundred Days of the 19th-century French emperor Napoleon.

individualism a political philosophy that argues that individuals are most effective when they are responsible only for their own well-being and not for that of other members of society.

installment buying a method of buying originally introduced by car companies in the 1920s that allowed purchasers to make a downpayment on a purchase and then pay the balance in a series of regular installments.

isolationism an approach adopted in the United States after World War I that argued that the country should disassociate itself from affairs elsewhere in the world. It led to the U.S. failure to join the League of Nations.

Keynesianism the economic theory advocated by John Maynard Keynes in the 1920s and 1930s. Keynes argued that governments should spend money to maintain full employment and stimulate the economy. His theories dominated most western democracies from the 1930s to around the 1980s.

labor union a formal organization in which workers act collectively in order to protect their interests such as pay and work conditions.

laissez-faire a French term for "let it be," used to describe an economy with no government regulation of business activity. Laissez-faire is an important part of classical or free-market economics, which holds that laws of supply and demand alone should regulate prices, wages, and other economic factors.

liberalism a political theory that emphasizes a belief in progress, the autonomy of individuals, and the protection of political and civil rights; also an economic theory based on competition and the free market.

mixed economy an economy that combines characteristics of a free-market economy—competition, private ownership—with a limited amount of state involvement, such as regulation of business, wage and hour legislation, and a degree of nationalization.

mutualism a U.S. political tradition that advocates cooperative action as a way to lessen the negative social effects of the economy. The mutualist tradition was behind the general acceptance in the 1930s that government had an obligation to look after its citizens.

nativism an anti-immigrant U.S. political tradition that values "real" Americans and their attitudes over those of more recent immigrants. In the late 19th century nativism saw first- or second-generation Irish immigrants objecting to newcomers from southern Europe, for example.

planned economy an economy in which economic activity is controlled by the state. Most businesses are nationalized rather than privately owned, and the government sets production quotas, wages, and prices.

populism a name given to numerous political movements of the 1930s that claimed to represent the common people; populism also describes the beliefs of the Populist Party formed in 1891 to represent rural interests and the breakup of monopolies.

progressivism a political tradition in the United States that advocated social reform by government legislation. Both the Republican and Democratic parties had progressive wings.

public works projects often large-scale projects run by federal, state, or local government in order to generate employment.

recession a severe decline in economic activity that lasts for at least six months

regulation a word used to describe moves by government or other agencies to control business activity, such as by legislation relating to minimum wages or maximum working hours or health and safety procedures.

relief the term most often used in the 1920s and 1930s for welfare.

Social Darwinism a social theory based on the theory of natural selection proposed by Charles Darwin. Social Darwinists believed that some people inevitably became richer or more powerful than others, and that inequality was therefore acceptable.

socialism a political doctrine that removes business from private ownership in favor of state or cooperative ownership in order to create a more equitable society.

welfare financial or other help distributed to people in need; the word is also sometimes used to apply to the agencies that distribute the aid.

FURTHER READING

Allen, Frederick Lewis. *Since Yesterday: The 1930s in America, September 3, 1929–September 3, 1939*. New York: HarperCollins, 1986.

Brogan, Hugh. *The Penguin History of the United States of America*. New York: Penguin Books, 1990.

Evans, Harold. *The American Century*. New York: Knopf, 1999.

Handlin, Oscar, and Lilian Handlin. *Liberty and Equality: 1920–1994*. New York: HarperCollins Publishers, 1994.

Jones, M. A. *The Limits of Liberty: American History 1607–1992*. New York: Oxford University Press, 1995.

Kennedy, David M. *Freedom From Fear: The American People in Depression and War, 1929–1945* (Oxford History of the United States). New York: Oxford University Press, 1999.

Meltzer, Milton. *Brother Can You Spare a Dime?: The Great Depression 1929–1933* New York: Facts on File, Inc., 1991.

Nardo, Don (ed.). *The Great Depression* (Opposing Viewpoints Digest). Greenhaven Press, 1998.

Parrish, Michael E. *Anxious Decades: America in Prosperity and Depression, 1920–1941*. New York: W. W. Norton & Company Inc., 1994.

Phillips, Cabell. *From the Crash to the Blitz: 1929-1939*. Bronx, NY: Fordham University Press, 2000.

Watkins, T. H. *The Great Depression: America in the 1930s*. Boston: Little Brown and Co, 1995.

Worster, Donald. *Dust Bowl: The Southern Plains in the 1930s*. New York: Oxford University Press, 1982

NOVELS AND EYEWITNESS ACCOUNTS

Agee, James, and Walker Evans. *Let Us Now Praise Famous Men*. Boston: Houghton Mifflin Co., 2000

Burg, David F. *The Great Depression: An Eyewitness History*. New York: Facts on File, Inc., 1996

Caldwell, Erskine. *God's Little Acre*. Athens, GA: University of Georgia Press, 1995.

Caldwell, Erskine, and Margaret Bourke-White. *You Have Seen Their Faces*. Athens, GA: University of Georgia Press, 1995.

Dos Passos, John. *U.S.A.* New York: Library of America, 1996.

Farell, James T. *Studs Lonigan: A Trilogy*. Urbana: University of Illinois Press, 1993.

Faulkner, William. *Absalom, Absalom!* Boston: McGraw Hill College Division, 1972.

Hemingway, Ernest. *To Have and Have Not*. New York: Scribner, 1996.
———. *For Whom the Bell Tolls*. New York: Scribner, 1995.

Le Sueur, Meridel. *Salute to Spring*. New York: International Publishers Co., Inc., 1977.

McElvaine, Robert S. *Down and Out in the Great Depression: Letters from the Forgotten Man*. Chapel Hill, NC: University of North Carolina Press, 1983.

Olsen, Tillie. *Yonnondio: From the Thirties*. New York: Delta, 1979.

Smedley, Agnes. *Daughter of Earth: A Novel*. New York: Feminist Press, 1987.

Steinbeck, John. *The Grapes of Wrath*. New York: Penguin USA, 1992.
———. *Of Mice and Men*. New York: Penguin USA, 1993.

Terkel, Studs. *Hard Times: An Oral History of the Great Depression*. New York: The New Press, 2000.

Wright, Richard. *Native Son*. New York: HarperCollins, 1989.

PROLOGUE TO THE DEPRESSION

Allen, Frederick Lewis. *Only Yesterday*. New York: Harper and Brothers, 1931.

Bordo, Michael D., Claudia Goldin, and Eugene N. White (eds.). *The Defining Moment: The Great Depression and the American Economy in the Twentieth Century*. Chicago: University of Chicago Press, 1998.

Cohen, Lizabeth. *Making a New Deal*. New York: Cambridge University Press, 1990.

Galbraith, John Kenneth. *The Great Crash 1929*. Boston: Houghton Mifflin Co., 1997.

Kennedy, David M. *Over Here: The First World War and American Society*. New York: Oxford University Press, 1980.

Knock, T. J. *To End All Wars: Woodrow Wilson and the Quest for a New World Order*. Princeton, NJ: Princeton University Press.

Levian, J. R. *Anatomy of a Crash, 1929*. Burlington, VT: Fraser Publishing Co., 1997.

Sobel, Robert. *The Great Bull Market: Wall Street in the 1920s*. New York: W. W. Norton & Company Inc., 1968.
———. *Panic on Wall Street*. New York: Macmillan, 1968.

Wilson, Joan Hoff. *Herbert Hoover: Forgotten Progressive*. Boston: Little, Brown, 1975.

FDR AND OTHER INDIVIDUALS

Alsop, Joseph. *FDR: 1882–1945*. New York: Gramercy, 1998.

Brinkley, Alan. *Voices of Protest: Huey Long, Father Coughlin, and the Great Depression*. New York: Knopf, 1982.

Cook, Blanche Wiesen. *Eleanor Roosevelt: A Life*. New York: Viking, 1992.

Fried, Albert, *FDR and His Enemies*. New York: St. Martin's Press, 1999.

Graham, Otis L., Jr., and Meghan Wander (eds.) *Franklin D. Roosevelt, His Life and Times: An Encyclopedic View*. Boston: G.K. Hall & Co, 1985.

Hunt, John Gabriel, and Greg Suriano (eds.). *The Essential Franklin Delano Roosevelt: FDR's Greatest Speeches, Fireside Chats, Messages, and Proclamations*. New York: Gramercy, 1998.

Maney, Patrick J. *The Roosevelt Presence: The Life and Legacy of FDR*. Berkeley: University of California Press, 1998.

Roosevelt, Eleanor. *The Autobiography of Eleanor Roosevelt*. New York: Da Capo Press, 2000.

Watkins, T. H. *Righteous Pilgrim: The Life and Times of Harold L. Ickes*. New York: Henry Holt, 1990.

White, Graham. *Harold Ickes of the New Deal: His Private Life and Public Career*. Cambridge, MA: Harvard University Press, 1985.

SOCIAL HISTORY

Clausen, John A. *American Lives: Looking Back at the Children of the Great Depression*. Berkeley, CA: University of California Press, 1995.

Elder, Glen H., Jr. *Children of the Great Depression*. New York: HarperCollins, 1998.

Gregory, James N. *American Exodus: The Dust Bowl Migration and Okie Culture in California*. New York: Oxford University Press, 1991.

Katz, Michael B. *In the Shadow of the Poorhouse: A Social History of Welfare in America*. New York: Basic Books, 1997.

Lowitt, Richard, and Maurine Beasley (eds.). *One Third of a Nation: Lorena Hickok Reports on the Great Depression*. Urbana: University of Illinois Press, 1981.

McGovern, James R. *And a Time for Hope: Americans and the Great Depression*. Westport, CT: Praeger Publishers, 2000.

Patterson, James T. *America's Struggle Against Poverty: 1900–1980*. Cambridge, MA: Harvard University Press, 1981.

Starr, Kevin. *Endangered Dreams: The Great Depression in California* (Americans and the California Dream). New York: Oxford University Press, 1996.

Ware, Susan. *Holding the Line: American Women in the 1930s.* Boston: Twayne, 1982.

Weiss, Nancy. *Farewell to the Party of Lincoln: Black Politics in the Age of FDR.* Princeton: Princeton University Press, 1983.

CULTURE AND THE ARTS

Benet's Reader's Encyclopedia of American Literature. New York: Harpercollins, 1996.

Davidson, Abraham A. *Early American Modernist Painting, 1910–1935.* New York: Da Capo Press, 1994.

Haskell, Barbara. *The American Century: Art & Culture, 1900–1950.* New York: W. W. Norton & Co., 1999.

Hughes, Robert. *American Visions: The Epic History of Art in America.* New York: Knopf, 1999.

McJimsey, George. *Harry Hopkins: Ally of the Poor and Defender of Democracy.* Cambridge, Mass.: Harvard University Press, 1987.

Meltzer, Milton. *Violins and Shovels: The WPA Arts Projects.* New York: Delacorte Press, 1976.

———. *Dorothea Lange: A Photographer's Life.* Syracuse, NY: Syracuse University Press, 2000.

Pells, R. H. *Radical Visions and American Dreams: Culture and Social Thought in the Depression Years.* Urbana: Illinios University Press, 1998.

Pollack, Howard. *Aaron Copland: The Life and Work of an Uncommon Man.* New York: Henry Holt & Co., Inc., 1999.

Thomson, David. *Rosebud: The Story of Orson Welles.* New York: Vintage Books, 1997.

Wilson, Edmond. *The American Earthquake: A Document of the 1920s and 1930s.* Garden City, NY: Doubleday, 1958.

INTERNATIONAL AFFAIRS

Bullock, Alan. *Hitler: A Study in Tyranny.* New York: Harper and Row, 1962.

Dallek, Robert. *Franklin D. Roosevelt and American Foreign Policy.* New York: Oxford University Press, 1979.

Kindleberger, Charles P. *The World in Depression, 1929–1939.* Berkeley: University of California Press, 1986.

Offner, A. A. *The Origins of the Second World War: American Foreign Policy and World Politics.* Melbourne, FL: Krieger Publishing Company, 1986.

Pauley, B. F. *Hitler, Stalin, and Mussolini: Totalitarianism in the Twentieth Century.* Wheeling, IL: Harlan Davidson, 1997.

Ridley, J. *Mussolini.* New York: St. Martin's Press, 1998.

WEB SITES

African American Odyssey: The Depression, The New Deal, and World War II
http://lcweb2.loc.gov/ammem/aaohtml/exhibit/aopart8.html

America from the Great Depression to World War II: Photographs from the FSA and OWI, 1935–1945
http://memory.loc.gov/ammem/fsowhome.html

The American Experience: Surviving the Dust Bowl
http://www.pbs.org/wgbh/amex/dustbowl

Biographical Directory of the United States Congress
http://bioguide.congress.gov

By the People, For the People: Posters from the WPA, 1936–1943
http://memory.loc.gov/ammem/wpaposters/wpahome.html

Federal Theater Project
http://memory.loc.gov/ammem/fedtp/fthome.html

Huey Long
http://www.lib.lsu.edu/special/long.html

The New Deal Network, Franklin and Eleanor Roosevelt Institute
http://newdeal.feri.org

New York Times Archives
http://www.nytimes.com

Presidents of the United States
http://www.ipl.org/ref/POTUS.html

The Scottsboro Boys
http://www.english.upenn.edu/~afilreis/88/scottsboro.html

Voices from the Dust Bowl: The Charles L. Todd and Robert Sonkin Migrant Worker Collection, 1940–1941
http://memory.loc.gov/ammem/afctshtml/tshome.html

WPA American Life Histories
http://lcweb2.loc.gov/ammem/wpaintro/wpahome.html

PICTURE CREDITS

TIMELINE OF THE DEPRESSION

1929
Hoover creates Farm Board
Stock-market crash (October)

1930
California begins voluntary repatriation of Mexicans and Mexican Americans
Smoot-Hawley Tariff Act
Little Caesar, first great gangster movie of the sound era
Ford cuts workforce by 70 percent (June)
Drought strikes Midwest (September)

1931
Credit Anstalt, Austrian bank, collapses (May 1)
All German banks close (July 13)
Britain abandons gold standard (September 21)

1932
Norris-La Guardia Act
Congress approves Reconstruction Finance Corporation (January 22)
FDR makes "forgotten man" radio broadcast (April 7)
Repression of Bonus Expeditionary Force by Douglas MacArthur (June 17)
Farmers' Holiday Association organizes a farmers' strike (August)
FDR wins a landslide victory in presidential election (November 8)

1933
Fiorello La Guardia elected mayor of New York City.
Nazi leader Adolf Hitler becomes chancellor of Germany
Assassination attempt on FDR by Giuseppe Zangara (February 15)
FDR takes oath as 32nd president of the United States (March 4)
National bank holiday (March 6)
Start of the Hundred Days: Emergency Banking Relief Act (March 9)
FDR delivers first "fireside chat" (March 12)
Economy Act (March 20)
Beer-Wine Revenue Act (March 22)
Civilian Conservation Corps Reforestation Relief Act (March 31)
Emergency Farm Mortgage Act (May)
Federal Emergency Relief Act (FERA) and Agricultural Adjustment Administration (AAA) created (May 12)
Tennessee Valley Authority (May 18)
Federal Securities Act (May 27)
London Economic Conference (June)
Home Owners Refinancing Act (June 13)
Banking Act; Farm Credit Act; Emergency Railroad Transportation Act; National Industrial Recovery Act;

Glass Steagall Banking Act (June 16)
73rd Congress adjourns (June 16)
FDR creates Civil Works Administration (November)

1934
U.S. joins International Labour Organization
Huey Long launches Share-Our-Wealth Society (January)
Farm Mortgage Refinancing Act (January 31)
Securities Exchange Act (June 6)
National Housing Act (June 28)

1935
Emergency Relief Appropriation Act (April 8)
Soil Conservation Act (April 27)
Resettlement Administration created (May 1)
Rural Electrification Administration created (May 11)
Sureme Court rules NIRA unconstitutional (May 27)
Works Progress Administration formed (May 6)
Federal Music Project introduced (July)
National Labor Relations (Wagner) Act (July 5)
Social Security Act (August 14)
Banking Act (August 23)
Public Utility Holding Company Act (August 28)
Farm Mortgage Moratorium Act (August 29)
Revenue Act of 1935 (August 30)
Wealth Tax Act (August 31)
Huey Long dies after assassination (September 10)

1936
FDR wins 1936 election (November 3)
Gone with the Wind published
Charlie Chaplin's *Modern Times* is last great silent movie
Supreme Court rules AAA unconstitutional (January 6)
Soil Conservation and Domestic Allotment Act (1936) (February 29)
Voodoo Macbeth opens in New York (April 14)

1937
Wagner-Steagall National Housing Act (September 1)
Supreme Court axes NLRB
CIO wins a six-week sit-down strike at General Motors plant in Flint, Michigan.
Supreme Court Retirement Act (March 1)
Bituminous Coal Act (April 26)
Neutrality Act of 1937 (May 1)
Farm Tenant Act (July 22)

Revenue Act of 1937 (August 26)
National Housing Act (September 1)
Start of sit-down strike at General Motors Fisher Body Plant in Flint, Michigan, which lasts 44 days (December)

1938
Amended Federal Housing Act (February 4)
Agricultural Adjustment Act (1938) (February 16)
Naval Expansion Act of 1938 (May 17)
Revenue Act of 1938 (May 28)
Food, Drink, and Cosmetic Act (June 24)
Fair Labor Standards Act (June 25)
Orson Welles' *The War of the Worlds* broadcast (October 30)

1939
John Steinbeck's *The Grapes of Wrath* published
Public Works Administration discontinued
Federal Loan Agency created
Supreme Court declares the sit-down strike illegal (February 27)
Administrative Reorganization Act of 1939 (April 3)
Hatch Act (August 2)
Outbreak of World War II in Europe (September 3)
Neutrality Act of 1939 (November 4)

1940
In California the Relief Appropriation Act is passed, raising the period of eligibility for relief from one to three years
Richard Wright's *Native Son* establishes him as the era's leading black author

1941
American Guide series published for the last time
Publication of James Agee and Walker Evans' *Let Us Now Praise Famous Men*
Japanese bomb Pearl Harbor, Hawaii, bringing U.S. into World War II (December 7)

1943
Government eliminates all WPA agencies

1944
Farm Security Administration closed

1945
FDR dies
Japanese surrender

INDEX